# MENTAL HEALTH CARE
## AT CHURCH AND BEYOND

# MENTAL HEALTH CARE
## AT CHURCH AND BEYOND

*by*
DR. B.R. REESE

**EQUIP PRESS**

*Colorado Springs*

# MENTAL HEALTH CARE
## AT CHURCH AND BEYOND

Scripture quotations marked (ESV) are taken from The ESV® Bible (The Holy Bible, English Standard Version®) copyright © 2001 by Crossway, a publishing minis-try of Good News Publishers. ESV® Text Edition: 2011. The ESV® text has been reproduced in cooperation with and by permission of Good News Publishers. Unauthorized reproduction of this publication is prohibited. Used by permission. All rights reserved.

Scripture quotations marked (KJV) are taken from the King James Bible. Accessed on Bible Gateway at www.BibleGateway.com.

Scripture quotations marked (NASB) are taken from the New American Standard Bible® (NASB), copyright © 1960, 1962, 1963, 1968, 1971, 1972, 1973, 1975, 1977, 1995 by The Lockman Foundation, www.Lockman.org. Used by permission.

Scripture quotations marked (NIV) are taken from the Holy Bible, New International Version. Copyright © 1973, 1978, 1984, 2011 by Biblica, Inc.® Used by permission. All rights reserved worldwide.

Scripture quotations marked (NKJV) are taken from the New King James Version®. Copyright © 1982 by Thomas Nelson, Inc. Used by permission. All rights reserved.

Scripture quotations marked (NLT) are taken from the Holy Bible, New Living Translation, copyright © 1996, 2004, 2015 by Tyndale House Foundation. Used by permission of Tyndale House Publishers, Inc., Carol Stream, Illinois 60188. All rights reserved.

Scripture quotations marked (NRSV) are taken from the New Revised Standard Version Bible, copyright © 1989 the Division of Christian Education of the National Council of the Churches of Christ in the United States of America. Used by permission. All rights reserved.

First Edition: Year 2018
Mental Health Care at Church and Beyond /Dr. B.R. Reese
Paperback ISBN: 978-1-946453-57-0
eBook ISBN: 978-1-946453-58-7

**EQUIP PRESS**

Colorado Springs

# PRAISE FOR
# MENTAL HEALTH CARE
# AT CHURCH AND BEYOND

African Americans experiencing psychological distress are more likely to seek help from a trusted clergy leader than any other group, and yet the Black Church is still lagging behind when it comes to mental health support. Pastors and ministry leaders are sadly still offering those experiencing mental health challenges quick solutions like "more prayer" and Scripture reading. Offering simple solutions to pressing issues perpetuates stigma and misconception of mental illness as a spiritual problem, due to lack of awareness.

So what do we do when "praying more" is not enough? Clergy leaders lacking basic knowledge of mental health should not attempt mental health counseling beyond offering referral services. African Americans have a difficult time finding mental health providers that align with the Christian faith and support their values and attitudes.

*Mental Health Care at Church and Beyond* offers best practices on how to engage African Americans through collaboration with faith-based organizations and mental health providers to decrease stigma, develop cultural competency, and improve access to mental health care. In addition, the author provides theological and sound evidence of mental health examples in the Bible.

Essentially, *Mental Health Care at Church and Beyond* acknowledges the role of the Black Church as a pillar in the African-American community and the necessity of life-affirming messages from the pulpit for African Americans and the broader community. This is a brilliant piece of work with the promise of providing help and facilitating healing for African Americans and the community-at-large.

— *Jameisha (Meisha) Brown,*
*PhD(c), M.S., CHES, Health Minister*

*My grace is sufficient for you, for power is made perfect in weakness. So, I will boast all the more gladly of my weaknesses, so that the power of Christ may dwell in me.* – 2 Corinthians 12:9

The confluence of faith and mental health is complex and unique to each individual. Giving God all the glory for our well-being does not relieve the faith community of its responsibility to address mental wellness. To the contrary, God calls us to build on the unique strengths of churches and church leaders to identify the need for behavioral resources and refer congregants (and pastoral leaders) to those local treatment providers and recovery support services that make us perfect in weakness. This book is a heartfelt call for an open conversation about perfection in weakness. Here, the reader will find the evidence-based approach and the action plan outline to address mental health recovery and wellness in our own congregations. LifeSteps has plans to launch a peer recovery support program, and this book will be an important part of understanding diversity when coaching people on their path to recovery.

— *Laurie Born, MPAff, ACPS, Executive Director,*
*LifeSteps Council on Alcohol and Drugs*

I have worked in the field of mental health for over twenty years and am now the Director for The Center of Counseling and Behavioral Health at The Potter's House of Dallas, Texas under the tutelage of Bishop T.D. Jakes. It is with extreme pleasure and honor that I recommend this book. I have seen first-hand Dr. Reese navigate life's complexities and maintain his hope, integrity, and faith in God. His life has equipped him to pen this poignant and inspiring work—a clarion call to others to keep reaching for wholeness despite difficult circumstances. Dr. Reese has a way of utilizing his unique wit combined with his spiritual insight to captivate the reader and take them on a healing and transformative journey. I encourage the reader to approach these written words with an open heart and mind and allow the balm of healing to flow into their lives.

I am convinced you will be enriched the author's transparency and realness as he shares his journey to wholeness. It is your time, your season to move forward and step into what God has for you, and I believe this book is a continuation of the blessings God has in store for you!

Natasha Stewart MA, Director for the Center of Counseling and Behavioral Health, The Potter's House of Dallas, Texas

Like Joshua, Rev. Dr. Billy Reese is commissioned by God to lead his flock to total mental well-being. With God, there is a renewing of the body, mind, and soul—there is abundant life. There is perfect peace. Yes, *mental health is a problem in the pews*. There is a growing body of sociological and psychological research interested in the effects of mental health in religion. This increasing literature argues there is a positive effect and influence when pastors care for and pray for their flock. Although clergy are often called upon to provide mental health pastoral care, their response to this mission remains relatively unexamined. Little is known about what clergy do when faced with mental health problems among their communities.

This book opens the door to what may become a richer, deeper conversation on issues of forgiveness, acceptance, gratitude, hope, and love. *Mental Health Care at Church and Beyond* is a safe, spiritual space for individuals and communities to reclaim their mental health care at church and beyond.

*— Dr. Anne Onyekwuluje, Professor of Sociology,*
*Western Kentucky University*

*Mental Health Care at Church and Beyond* creates an excellent opportunity for those who are faith-driven to begin to understand the complexities of health and wellness in themselves and in their communities. Through the lens of Pastor B.R. Reese's vast experience at the pulpit in leading community resource initiatives in his local community, he has shed light on new ways of thinking about the impacts of mental health for pastors and their congregation. In meeting with the Wellness and Empowerment Community Ministries at God's Way Baptist Church, I have witnessed how Pastor Reese and others have begun addressing the needs of the congregants through initiatives that have focused on the African-American community in Taylor, Texas. Lastly, this book addresses the opportunity to explore the concepts of self-care for those who are leading churches and faith-based organizations and initiatives. I would recommend this book as a great resource and conversation starter for those working in the mental health and pastoral communities.

*— Ray Langlois, Principal Consultant,*
*Langlois Consultant Services, LLC*

Dr. Reese serves is a beautiful model of a safe sanctuary for all. In *Mental Health Care at Church and Beyond*, he educates and equips congregations to engage in mental health ministry. He recognizes the critical role that churches play in the rural and African American experience and the urgent need to equip them to heal rather than hurt. He uses the Word of God to show divine evidence of mercy and tenderness for persons with mental illness. It is a call to action for churches to offer humanity and grace to persons experiencing mental illness and their family members. With that call, Dr. Reese extends his hand and offers the reader tools to answer that call.

— *Jennie Birkholz, Principal,*
*Breakwater Light, Texas Faith and Health Network*

What struck me most in reading Dr. Billy Reese's book was his compassion in the stories and in the strategies he suggests for his fellow pastors and the rest of us. It is sometimes a struggle to find compassion in one's heart when those who suffer mental and behavioral health issues wound us. The Bible and sacred books of many religions extol us to be compassionate. But it can be hard, not just for the parents, spouses, children, and friends of those who suffer mental and behavioral health issues, but for those who offer support as well.

*And the Lord said, I will cause all my goodness to pass in front of you, and I will proclaim my name, the Lord, in your presence. I will have mercy, and I will have compassion on whom I will have compassion.*
– Exodus 33:19

The stories and strategies offered in this book allude to kindness and sympathy for those who struggle. There are big expectations set upon the pastors and reverends who willingly serve as God's first responders. There are lessons for all of us in this book about compassion and the power of God's love and healing. This book shares something profoundly powerful in helping us understand the meaning and significance of compassion. In Latin, the origin of the word "compati" means to "suffer with." True compassion is not an easy thing, and it often means someone's pain becomes your own. Learning compassion is a grace note that can change your life.

*— Deborah Vollmer Dahlke, DrPH, CEO/President*
*DVD Associates, LLC, Adjunct Associate Professor,*
*TX A&M School of Public Health, Faculty Associate,*
*TX A&M Center for Population Health and Aging*

Historically, the church as an institution, whether large or small, has ignored mental health illness. The result is that this renders an often-tragic impact on the church and its members. This work by Pastor Reese provides a systematic approach that helps build the necessary resources for support in the local church. It is an outstanding treatise, and we believe that this will become the workhorse manual and tool for Pastors throughout the US. We must utilize this discussion to bring forth the manifestation of the Holy Spirit that brings about the re-emergence of members to full personhood, which God endorses henceforth and forever.

*— Preston J. Allen, MDiv., MA, Director for Nonprofits*
*at Wheeler Avenue Baptist Church, Houston, Texas*

*Mental Health at Church and Beyond* is a unique book that can help pastors, families, and community members understand mental health from the perspective of the clergy. Clergy is not often transparent regarding their initial misinterpretations of mental health. Dr. Reese encourages readers to understand that healing, compassion, and spirituality is for all. Addressing mental health is difficult in faith communities because many wrestle with stigma, shame, and misunderstanding. I am elated that Dr. Reese's book will open dialogue with clergy.

*Mental Health Care at Church and Beyond* is a brilliant work, and the author will enlighten, inspire, and captivate readers to embrace and build healthy relationships with individuals with mental health.

I have worked in the field of disabilities for more than twenty years, and this book would have been helpful during my career.

— *Sonya Hosey, BSW*

# CONTENTS

# ACKNOWLEDGMENTS

First and foremost, all thanks be unto God and Jesus Christ, our Savior and Lord who has caused all grace to abound in all things. Blessings to all the pastors and church leaders for their leadership and unwavering support of emotional and mental health care.

A special thank you to Associate Pastor Sonya Hosey, Minister Eugenia Kleinpeter, Nicole Traphan, Lady Debora Taylor, and Pastor Larry Taylor for their wisdom and knowledge of the need to further enhance awareness and education of mental health issues within churches and communities—outstanding work. A thank you to Jennie Brikholz Stuart for her creative effort in connecting faith-based initiatives regarding mental health and emotional well-being.

A special thank you to Rhonda Franklin Romar and Nicole Traphan for sharing stories about themselves and their families with conviction. Their stories demonstrate that there is hope for all of us to overcome our daily struggles. Their willingness to be transparent is a testimony within itself of their love for Jesus, and others.

A special thank you to Josephine Gurch for writing her blog, a weekly digest of news in Texas and beyond—"The rural church creating inclusion through education"—here at God's Way Christian Baptist Church, Taylor Texas.

I want to thank Life Steps, Bluebonnet Trails Community Services, and a special thanks to the Hogg Foundation for its support in providing the opportunity to bring mental health awareness to rural America and beyond.

I certainly want to thank God's Way Christian Baptist Church for its leadership role, active participation in mental health education, and compassionate love.

A special thanks to my wife, Dollie Reese, for her love and compassion in caring for numerous children in foster care, touching and changing the lives of so many.

We are thankful for the Hogg Foundation Mental Health (MH), an African American Faith-Based Initiative, and their unwavering support to African American churches in taking the lead in bringing about mental health awareness to many.

Thanks to everyone who has contributed to the edification of this book. I truly appreciate you for your labor of work and love. Together, we are making a difference. Certainly, we thank God for the community of pastors, church leaders, and professional staff members who are making a difference as we continue to address the problem of mental health within our churches.

# INTRODUCTION

*W*hat is mental health? MentalHealth.gov defines it as our emotional, psychological, and social well-being. It affects how we think, feel, and act. It is the ability to function effectively in daily activities, resulting in productivity at playful activities, work, and school; experiencing fulfilling relationships; and developing resilience to change and adversity. Mental health is important at every stage of life, from childhood and adolescence through adulthood.

I hope every pastor will accept the challenge to learn more about mental health and how to engage in the care of congregants. Mental health is a shared responsibility, and it is ok to make referrals for professional help—the burden doesn't rest upon their shoulders alone. We are all keepers one of another.

It's ok to walk beside our congregants while being ministered to by professional care providers. It is all a part of the total process of healing that has God's approval, as revealed in the Good Samaritan story in the Bible, where the innkeeper is classified as a professional care provider. We just need to understand the follow-up and the follow-through of ministry, especially around mental health issues.

As pastors and professional care providers, we all must address the needs of those suffering in silence, feeling hopeless and helpless because of the help and support needed. A vital part of the pastoral team is to provide care and support and always be aware of congregant discrimination as it relates to emotional and mental health concerns. Later I will discuss church therapy, the practice of inclusion, and the way to wellness among congregants.

Many parishioners are afraid to disclose their mental trauma struggles to anyone in their local congregations. They fear rejection or even judgment while being authentic in describing their struggles. We must learn to hear the voice around mental health in a caring way.

Our plan here at God's Way is to develop an emotionally healthy church. I felt led and challenged by the Lord to write about mental health care and the need for more pastors and church leaders to take a more active role. To address the mental health issues of congregants within our local churches and beyond, the pastor or church leader are vital team players. The objective is to bring about total awareness and inclusion for everyone to be acknowledged as a gifted member in the body of Christ. My prayer is that every pastor/leader will accept the challenge to address mental health. Throughout the book, you will discover ways to have a healthier, stigma-free church.

You will discover that there are many tools and techniques with points of interest that can be helpful in addressing mental health within our local church and beyond—tools to build a safer place of worship and shared responsibilities in worship and service, tools to inform, instruct, and educate pastors and church leaders on how to better understand and support those who are struggling with mental and emotional issues where we live and worship.

This book intends to point out that every church has a dialogue around mental health awareness, a designed model health plan, and its message can be shared from the pulpit. Designed programs or helpful workshops, and where people meet, such as barbershops or community group initiatives engaged in mental health concerns, are all a part of a support group.

There are stories of people with experience sharing their journey while living with mental health. Powerful empowerment tools are also included that are helpful in managing daily struggles and eliminating the stigma that seems to plague so many. Also included is the evidence of techniques that have helped them live a better day and many talking points as starters to help frame those discussions around mental health.

We will take a closer look at what church life should look like around mental health. Every church should take the challenge to determine whether it is healthy enough to tackle mental health issues. Scripture is used throughout because real people in those days had real struggles. Bible stories center on the then and now of mental health, people of like passion. Survivors speak volumes of truth that mental health has always existed within the spiritual realm of believers, and it's ok to talk.

I believe every church ought to have a mental health model plan, where Christ is modeled and centered on all we do at church for the edification and upbuilding of the body of Christ. The chapters ahead offer nuggets that should have everyone talking about mental health among congregants, family members, and our neighbors. We will discover a better way to support and encourage those we love.

The objective is to bring about mental health awareness, offer more educational programs among congregants, discuss how to address mental health at church, and help develop a mental health model that serves everyone, even in the worship experience. It is a call for diversity and total inclusion.

Stigma can be a sensitive and touchy topic; therefore, we should beware of languages, words used inappropriately that can be damaging and lead to further traumatization, neglect, and daily struggles that occur within our local churches and beyond. I want to sing to and beat the drums. Because God is not a respecter of persons, we do not discriminate when choosing with whom to fellowship.

We often preach that Heaven is a prepared place for a prepared people, especially for those who have accepted Jesus as both Savior and Lord. In that great day, people from all walks of life will be partakers, and there will be no discrimination.

We hope that those experiencing mental health or depression will feel safe in our churches and sense that they are a part of integral care and can experience a better life.

There is obviously a God Answers Prayer (G.A.P.) story evolving around mental health. The churched send a silent cry regarding mental health out into our midst. The human cry is, "I am over here alone, separated and hoping to feel, hear, or even see a better day."

From a pastor's perspective, let's look deep into our congregant's eyes and take a moment to care, a teachable moment indeed. We will sense a more holistic need beyond a spiritual outcry for immediate help.

One must conclude that there are unspoken words, such as, "Pastor, where now shall I go, and how can I survive here? It's a Macedonian call for help and is a church issue that needs addressing in church business meetings. Mental Health is a problem in the pews.

There is a mental health stigma sweeping across American and beyond. It is inevitable that mental health issues are in our churches, and disproportionately present as well, and must be addressed with both spiritual and professional helps.

Statistics have proven that one out of every five congregants sitting in church is suffering in silence with a mental health or emotional issue that needs our support, love, and immediate attention.

As I was sitting at my desk looking at a LifeWay Recourse pamphlet, I ran across this article that got my attention about mental health at church among pastors. Bob Smietana provides vital information in a LifeWay research paper, answering the question, "How often do pastors speak to their churches in sermons or large group messages about mental health?"

The results were as follows:

- Several times a month – 3 percent
- About once a month – 4 percent
- Several times a year – 26 percent
- Once a year or rarely/never – 66 percent

If these facts are true in our worship service, those suffering with mental health truly sense the need for inclusion. Do I belong, is this a safe place, where do I fit in, what am I to do, or where do I go from here? See me.

As pastors and church leaders who serve as first responders to the people of God, we must conclude that no one care provider can address or solve the mental health problem alone. As pastors and professional care providers, we must work in concert with our faith-based and community partners to provide a more holistic approach to mental health care for our congregants and those beyond.

From a spiritual standpoint, mental health must be seen as a more unified initiative that involves other team players to totally support those who may be suffering from mental health, emotional wellness, or depression, which covers a broader perspective of general needs.

We understand G.A.P. as God Answers Prayer, and yes, that is true. But it's also true that God Answers our Personal needs, and He certainly cares for His own. He loves and cares for everyone personally who may be suffering from mental illness or depression disorders while serving God. It is a church story about who we really are and how compassionate we are with our congregants suffering from mental health issues.

Yes, congregants are worshiping in a spirit-filled setting at church while they are depressed, while being engaged with a family member who just doesn't know who to talk to or where to go for immediate help. It is our responsibility to step up and comfort those around us during their moments of distress. It's time to talk.

In an article, Pastor Rick Warren stated, "I'm not ok, you are not ok, but it's ok because God is ok." What a true statement. We all need some "me" time and time for self-care. Yes, even pastors need self-care and should expect someone to look in on them as well.

In his blog, Ed Stetzer mentioned that one in four pastors struggle with mental health. I believe this sheds a great light on the pulpit. Pastors are preaching while depressed and ministering under the anointing to help others who are suffering emotionally and mentally.

In her book, *Troubled Minds*, Amy Simpson discusses the things we don't like to talk about. The trauma and stigma of mental illness are real, and we should not pretend it doesn't exist. Everyone needs to talk about the impact of emotional and mental illness and how we should respond appositely.

Jared Pingleton of Focus on the Family says people with mental illness feel that the church doesn't care, and they feel left out. Pastors need more guidance and preparation for dealing with a mental health crisis.

And Bob Smietana in his blog shares a profound story entitled "Mental Illness Remains a Taboo Topic for Many Pastors and Congregants." It discusses why pastors are reluctant to talk about mental illness and share their struggles. From the pulpit to the pews, there is a need for transparency that opens doors for congregants to feel empowered to serve as an integral part of inclusion within church ministry, bringing closure to what I call the G.A.P. theory.

I felt lead to write about the message from the pulpit as a necessity to address mental health and have a more holistic dialogue about mental health within the church life.

To remove the stigma around mental health, I suggest some key starting points as an icebreaker to help balance the conversation among all congregants. I encourage pastors and leaders to have in place a forum for conversation and learning that is constructive, respectful, and intentional in addressing the overall purpose of having a model mental program that supports the needs of their congregants.

Without diversity, we can never be complete or whole. To address the concerns around mental health, there must be diversity and inclusion within the four walls of the church. First, we must make sure to involve every congregant, working toward creating a fair and equal worshiping environment that will be conducive to building a safer and better place of worship. It must become one of the core values of the church for everyone.

Both the churched and unchurched need our support and care. In Matthew 11:28-30, Jesus Himself asks us who may be weary and heavy laden to come to Him and He would give rest. Philippians 4:6-7 states, "Do not be anxious about anything, but in everything by prayer and supplication with thanksgiving let your requests be made known to God. And the peace of God, which surpasses all understanding, will guard your hearts and your minds in Christ Jesus." This is a personal invitation that has been extended to everyone who has a specific need, understanding that God truly answers prayer.

We must acknowledge the unwavering support of the Dallas and Houston churches that shared with us surmountable information on emotional and mental health. We thank Prairie View A/M University for assessments to help keep us on task.

Numerous volunteers and our partnering faith-based organizations have come together to help bring about a better day and say, "We care too." Again, thanks for the team support.

This initiative has allowed WECM and our faith partners to provide education, awareness, and support to families and persons with lived experiences to reduce the stigma and shame of mental health in the African American community as they enhance their overall spiritual well-being and health.

As we strive to continue to reach out and support those who may be suffering from mental health, emotional well-being, or depression, we understand that sustainability is vital for the cause. As we continue to bring mental health awareness to churches and communities at large, we thank you in advance for your support and prayers as we continue to bring awareness, support, and inclusion to all in an atmosphere of genuine love. Please feel free to visit us at gwcbctw.org, email us at gwcbctw@yahoo.com, or write us at God's Way Christian Baptist Church, P.O. Box 449 Taylor, Texas 76574. We would love to hear from you. Please share your stories with us and help us grow and learn as we minister to the needs of God's people.

Wellness and Empowerment Community Ministries (WECM) has built partnerships with families, clergy, and health entities in rural east Williamson County to educate about mental health, recovery, and wellness to reduce stigma and identify local behavioral health resources for treatment and support. Together we are stronger.

Building a bridge to mental health requires work, patience, teamwork, and, indeed, a compassionate spirit. Pastors and leaders, city officials, community leaders, health care providers, and caretakers are all part of the integral care for team building to provide and support mental health. We now have access to many resources that will help bridge the gap. I believe every church needs a mental health plan, and I am certain some have these things programmed in their ministry helps.

I am certain that there should be a continuous dialogue among spiritual leaders, mental health educators, and professional health providers. We must talk, we must engage, we must learn, we must be involved pastor to pastor and people to people, we are bridging the gap. Spiritual leaders are connecting with professional support as part of our team support system to better support and serve all that we should love and support.

Our mission is to bring about awareness and perceptions of mental health, recovery, and wellness in African American communities, churches, and beyond. We aim to educate and inform local pastors about mental health and how we as leaders can serve our congregants in a more holistic manner respectful to everyone within our ministries. Through empowerment, no one is left behind.

Our goal is to retain and share information and current updates on mental health concerns, that the local church would be thoroughly furnished to meet the everyday need of someone who may be struggling with mental health problems.

We believe when pastors and leaders are informed about mental illness, the road to recovery is possible for those in our family, our church, and our community. We believe the pastor role is a vital part of the plan for ministry helps. We need the leadership of pastors to embrace and encourage spiritual and mental support, acknowledging the need to share responsibilities with professional helps, such as referrals, as the need arises.

We must start by being educated and knowledgeable about mental health. Mental Health First Aid Training for Pastors and Church Leaders is a good starting point for awareness and involvement concerning mental health issues. As leaders, we are challenged to have a balanced approach to a variety of issues that are real and challenging to our congregants.

We all desire wellness, but what does that look like? There are many dimensions to wellness: spiritual, emotional, financial, social, physical, occupational, intellectual, and environmental. I believe that covers almost all of us and everything associated with mankind.

At church, certain problems require a certain degree of learning and attention: marital problems, hunger, homelessness, joblessness, lack of transportation, emotional problems, numerous health issues, and, of course, salvation. Well, mental health should also be part of the inclusion package.

As leaders, we are empowered to spiritually lead, support, discuss, and respond to every human cry. This is our calling to fulfill—we must minister to the whole person. Most leaders are called to be people persons; there is no place for antisocialism, especially in the church.

Our goal is to engage our communities and professional care providers to have open forums for discussion and intervention to address the stigma associated with mental illness and equality. Integrated professional helps serve as empowerment tools to support our effort in supporting our families and communities with mental health issues.

Many today within our congregations and beyond are suffering in silence with mental illness. We all know someone who may be affected by mental illness. As pastors, church leaders, community leaders, and professional care providers, we need to step up now.

It is time for all believers to become unified in their efforts to educate, inform, support, and work together in addressing the issues of mental health in a more proactive manner. It's true we might all be in the same room, even the same church or a health care summit, but we can't know what the stakeholder is offering until we talk. It's time to talk.

This book, *Mental Health Care at Church and Beyond*, is designed as a reference tool to bring about awareness, information, insight, and biblical knowledge. Its purpose is to intentionally get everyone involved. No one should suffer alone. The Bible says we are our brother's keeper; therefore, no one should ever walk alone, especially those who need our love, support, and compassionate spirit. No one should be left alone, especially at church.

The book furthers instructs us to surround ourselves with a support system, especially those who have our best interest at heart and truly care about our well-being. To encourage the faith community, as well as professional care providers, we can work together to help lighten the load as bearers of hope, with no distraction regarding spiritual beliefs.

The book certainly is not a professional counseling tool but serves to enlighten us to be more like Jesus in our Christian service. There is a need to support everyone who asks of us, especially at church, the household of faith.

We hope that this book serves as a sustainability for WECM. Our mission is to continue to bring about mental health awareness, to offer training programs, assist in referrals, to inform pastors, offer continued education, sponsor mental health conferences, and to further engage a healthier dialogue around mental health.

We aim to create total awareness, offer support, and educate congregants about how to be helpful and be mindful of how we often stigmatize those suffering mental illness within our local churches and beyond. The book only contains spiritually driven material that supports the need to be our brother's keepers. Any form of mental health diagnostics should be considered professional care provider decisions.

Our mission is to remove the stigma within the local church that has wrongly plagued so many. We must normalize mental health as any other disease that needs our attention so that we all may know the truth, and the truth will set many free. There has been a church barrier around mental health for far too long.

It's time to get past fatal distractions and the unnecessary self-inflicted problems regarding mental health within the church. There is room for spiritual maturity, diversity, and inclusion for all.

# CHAPTER ONE

# MENTAL HEALTH AWARENESS AT CHURCH

*M*ental health awareness begins with pastoral leadership. Statistics show that in church leadership, there is little participation or concern about providing mental health care for its congregants.

Many surveys have been taken about pastoral care and mental health problems within the local church. They revealed that neglect, denial, or even stagnation in mental health support is often present. Within the concentric circle of things, mental health is the least observed.

In her book, *Troubled Minds*, Amy Simpson shares her survey about dealing with mental illness in the church.

- 44.5 percent of church leaders are approached two to five times a year for help dealing with mental illness in the church.
- When church people are on medication or diagnosed with mental illness, over a third of them keep the matter private.

About 29.1 percent said that, on average, mental illness is never mentioned in sermons at their church.

- 40 percent of church leaders have never reached out to and ministered to a family within their congregation who has a mental illness.
- Approximately 80 percent of church leaders said they believe mental illness is real, treatable, and manageable.
- Mental illness can be caused by genetic, biological, or environmental factors.
- Only one 12.5 percent said mental illness is discussed in a healthy way in their church.

In his publication, "Mental Illness Remains Taboo Topic for Many Pastors," Bob Smietana shares with church leaders that there is not enough support for mental health within our local churches across America. According to the National Alliance on Mental Illness, one in four Americans suffers from mental illness in any given year. Many look to their church for spiritual guidance in times of distress, but they're unlikely to find much help on Sunday mornings. Bob also mentioned that 66 percent of Protestant senior pastors seldom speak to their congregation about mental illness.

That includes 39 percent who rarely speak and 10 percent who never speak about mental illness. About 16 percent of pastors speak about mental illness once a year. And 22 percent of pastors are reluctant to help those who suffer from acute mental illness because it takes too much time.

Those are among the findings of a recent study of faith and mental illness by the Nashville-based LifeWay Research. The study, co-sponsored by Focus on the Family, was designed to help churches better assist those affected by mental illness.

We certainly acknowledge that this information has been very helpful to local churches across America. We are thankful for the researchers, helpful publications, and so many other contributors that share their personal stories and studies about emotional and mental wellness. We are truly grateful to them and credit them for what we have learned from them. It has been vital in bringing about awareness of mental health needs in the local church and beyond.

Researchers looked at three groups for the study. They surveyed 1,000 senior Protestant pastors about how their churches approach mental illness. Researchers then surveyed 355 Protestant Americans diagnosed with an acute mental illness. They had either moderate to severe depression, bipolar, or schizophrenia. Among them were 200 churchgoers.

A third survey polled 207 Protestant family members of people with acute mental illness. Researchers also conducted an in-depth interview with 15 experts on spirituality and mental illness.

The study found pastors and churches want to help those who experience mental illness, but those good intentions don't always lead to action. People who suffer from mental illness often turn to pastors for help. Evaluations and surveys from Prairie View A/M University project that must be more involvement and support in African American churches and beyond around the mental health awareness initiative, especially across rural America.

We have found that most pastors need more guidance and preparation for dealing with mental health crises. They often don't have a plan to help individuals or families affected by mental illness and miss opportunities to be the church who cares for her own.

A summary of findings includes what researchers call key disconnects, including:

- 27 percent of churches have a plan to assist families affected by mental illness, according to pastors. And only 21 percent of family members are aware of a plan in their church.

- Only 14 percent of churches have a counselor skilled in mental illness on staff, and 13 percent train leaders on how to recognize mental illness, according to pastors.

- 68 percent of pastors say their church maintains a list of local mental health resources for church members. But only 28 percent of families are aware those resources exist.

- Family members (65 percent) and those with mental illness (59 percent) want their church to talk openly about mental illness, so the topic will not be taboo. But 66 percent of pastors speak to their church once a year or less on the subject.

This silence can leave people feeling ashamed or embarrassed about mental illness, said Jared Pingleton, director of counseling services at Focus on the Family. Those with mental illness can feel left out, as if the church doesn't care. Or worse, they can feel mental illness is a sign of spiritual failure.

We can talk about diabetes, heart attacks, asthma, and all sorts of other medical conditions, but mental illness is somehow seen as a lack of faith or a sin-related issue.

Most pastors say they know people who have been diagnosed with mental illness. Fifty-nine percent have counseled people who were later diagnosed. And pastors themselves aren't immune. Twenty-three percent of pastors say they've experienced mental illness, while 12 percent say they received a diagnosis for a mental health condition.

But those pastors are often reluctant to share their struggles, said Chuck Hannaford, a clinical psychologist and president of Heart Life Professional

Soul-Care in Germantown, Tennessee. He was one of the experts interviewed for the project. His book, *Picking Up the Pieces Handbook*, is a resourceful tool for ministry.

Hannaford counsels pastors in his practice and said many, if they have a mental illness like depression or anxiety, won't share that information with the congregation. He doesn't think pastors should share all the details of their diagnosis, but they could acknowledge they struggle with mental illness. "You know it's a shame that we can't be more open about it," he told researchers. "But what I'm talking about is just an openness from the pulpit that people struggle with these issues and it's not an easy answer."

Those with mental illness can also be hesitant to share their diagnosis at church. Michael Lyles, an Atlanta-based psychiatrist, says more than half his patients come from an evangelical Christian background. Most of them have told no one in their church what they were going through, including their pastors and small group leaders.

Ed Stetzer said what appears to be missing in most church responses is "an open forum for discussion and intervention that could help remove the stigma associated with mental illness. The stigma will only cease to exist when people are valued for who they are. Churches talk openly about cancer, diabetes, heart attacks, and other health conditions – they should do the same for mental illness, to reduce the sense of stigma."

Researchers asked those with mental illness about their experience in church:

- 10 percent say they've changed churches because of how a specific church responded to their mental illness.
- 13 percent either stopped attending church (8 percent) or could not find a church (5 percent).

- 37 percent answered "don't know" when asked how their church's reaction to their illness affected them.
- Among regular churchgoers with mental illness, 52 percent say they have stayed at the same church. 15 percent changed churches, while 8 percent stopped going to church, and 26 percent said, "Don't know."
- 53 percent say their church has been supportive. About 13 percent say their church was not supportive 33 percent answered "don't know" when asked if their church was supportive.

LifeWay Research also asked open-ended questions about how mental illness has affected people's faith. Those without support from the church said they struggled.

"My faith has gone to pot, and I have so little trust in others," one respondent told researchers.

"I have no help from anyone," said another respondent.

But others found support when they told their church about their mental illness.

"Several people at my church (including my pastor) have confided that they too suffer from mental illness," said one respondent.

"Reminding me that God will get me through and to take my meds," said another.

Mental illness, like other chronic conditions, can feel overwhelming at times, said Pingleton. Patients can feel as if their diagnosis defines their life. But that's not how the Bible sees those with mental illness, he said.

He pointed out that many biblical characters suffered from emotional struggles. And some, were they alive today, would likely be diagnosed with mental illness.

The Bible is filled with people who struggled with suicide or were depressed or bipolar. David was bipolar, and Elijah probably was as well. We don't remember them for those things—we remember them for their faith walk with God. With God, they never lost their purpose in ministry and their ability to serve.

# CHAPTER TWO

# THE PASTOR AS MENTAL HEALTH VISIONARY

As pastors, we must look in depth at many things concerning the will of God for His people. Mental health is one of those topics we cannot overlook or underestimate. We must take a more active role within the local church. Our vision and mission is to develop an emotionally healthy church conducive to the well-being of every believer and the ability to serve where God has called them.

When leaders can be visionary, visible, and vocal in sharing stories of their own recovery or experiences, it supports others and something powerful begins to happen. When leaders fight for the mental wellness of people who follow them, they can ignite the fire of hope others need to survive.

There is always a risk in anything we do—success always demands a calculated risk. It is often the price of freedom or release. The reward of leading the way through this dark side of life is so great and can be a special moment in someone's life. It's ok to share your story.

Some are suffering in silence within our pews and in the pulpit, and within our personal families and beyond. It has been reported that 85 percent of African Americans have been identified as using their faith to address their mental health needs. One in five people sitting in the pews have a mental issue and need our attention and full support. Most African Americans refuse to engage in professional helps such as counseling and medications. Most African American males refuse to have regular checkups.

Mental health issues are current and profound. The struggle is real. Many congregations seldom hear a message of encouragement and hope about mental health care support from the pulpit. Some churches do not have a mental health plan at church, some do have a plan that offers some assistant but no knowledge of resources. In a broader sense, stigmas are popping up everywhere within the church. Too many pastors are in denial when it comes to the responsibility of the church and her role in addressing mental health for the benefit of all congregants.

Churches in rural American seldom discuss mental health issues and the disparity beyond. Inclusion demands that everyone have access to mental health resources and receive the support needed to live a better life.

Most pastors are overbooked and extremely busy, but part of their agenda is to immediately address mental health issues. The rural or metropolitan church should be involved in addressing the mental health needs of their congregants. The conversation within our four walls constantly creates a stigma of what they call the mentally disturbed: the homeless, hurricane victims, and every-day beggars like Lazarus and blind Bartimaeus who no one thought enough of to tell them that Jesus of Nazareth was passing by. There are no second-class congregants in the kingdom of God.

Most mental health conversations are more harmful than good. Numerous congregants, along with extended family members and friends, live with an illness. They know firsthand the stigma that other congregants and members in society have created in speaking unkind words and distancing themselves. Often that distance can be created by both sides, the mentally sound and the person suffering from a mental illness. The church has much to learn in this area of spiritual helps.

If teaching and preaching are to be relevant to the full depth of the human cry of our day, it is expedient that sermons and teachings must deal with both mental health and emotional well-being just as with any other church-related issue, along with spiritual health.

Pastors, in general, can offer the most care and love from the pulpit. There are many individual needs that should be addressed from the pulpit with a clear message of hope and understanding. Congregant responsibility is vital to eliminate the stigma around mental health at church. Member participation with the pastor supports that, indeed, could be burden-lifting for many pastors who have multiple tasks that need immediate attention.

Statistically proven, members of the clergy are the **first contacts** for people who seek help for mental illness. You might wonder why people with this sort of problem keep finding their way to you and your church, of all places. There are a variety of reasons, including a mental health care system that is notoriously difficult to access and expects people with brain-based disorders to manage their own care through that system. Other reasons are inherent as it relates to the nature of faith communities: They offer spiritual experiences, promises of peace and love, opportunities for community, and for communion with God. These are understandably attractive to many people with mental illness. Therefore, church leaders are often first responders consciously or unconsciously.

Yet many pastors feel underequipped to respond. The good news is, resources are available. Most pastors and church leaders are not mental health experts, but that doesn't have to take away the challenge and heartbreak of ministry to people in serious pain. But learning to work together with the experts will help us understand what people are up against, what they need, and how the church can help. Not every church has an open-door policy for mental health needs.

The challenging question for leaders and congregants is whether anyone is suffering in silence in your church or feels comfortable enough to welcome you into their space. Is there an opportunity or open-door policy that enables them to share their story?

Jesus extends an opportunity for everyone to receive what He has for us. "Behold, I stand at the door, and knock: if any man hears my voice, and open the door, I will come in to him, and will sup with him, and he with me" (Revelation 3:20). That's irresistible grace and mercy extended to all. Mental health is one of the doors we must minister through as well.

Jesus stands at the door, but He can see through the door. He can see into our minds and hearts in-depth, He knows our every need. Jesus, as He stands at the door knocking, can see inside our hurting condition and offers unconditional love and compassion.

Standing there at the door, He sees a child sitting in the home in rage and anger. He sees a mother sitting in the home abused because of a violent husband. He sees a father sitting in the home upset because he has been jobless too long. He sees a Christian sitting in church saved but depressed, singing in the choir but depressed, preaching in the pulpit depressed.

Yes, at times, Jesus stands and knock at the church door and He sees a pastor standing in the pulpit preaching but depressed, suffering from emotional wars and experiencing member depression. Most pastors across rural America suffer from member depression, a common overload of responsibilities and everyday challenges, and a combination of both church and community needs, which can be overwhelming.

We must learn how to address mental illness in our churches and accept the responsibility that ministry is inclusive to all. We must have an honest dialogue among pastors, church leaders, congregants, and beyond.

At this point, it is obvious that so many people of faith are too ashamed, guilty, or embarrassed to risk making known their struggles with mental illness. Where there is no vision of mental health concerns, the people perish. Many feel alienated and angry because of poor pastoral care at church and have experienced a disconnect from participating in activities. Not everything we have said or done in the past concerning mental health was handled in a healthy way.

There is a need for vision planning that continues to educate pastors and congregants about mental health, to know there are various forms of healing and volumes of knowledge at our disposal about how mental health is defined. People can experience diverse types of mental health problems. These problems can affect your thinking, mood, and behavior. The pastoral care team should know that clinical depression involves physical symptoms such as mood swings, erratic behaviors, overeating, sleep disorders, isolation, hyper activities and so forth.

Many people think mental disorders are rare. But in fact, they are common. over 60 million Americans (1 in 4 adults) experience mental illness in a given year. In addition, 1 in 10 children lives with a serious mental or emotional disorder, mostly anxiety related.

Mental illnesses cause mild to significant disturbances in thinking, behavior, and/or emotion, resulting in an inability to cope with ordinary life challenges and routines. According to Mental Health America, there are more than 200 classified forms of mental illness. Some of the more common disorders are depression, bipolar disorder, dementia, schizophrenia, and anxiety disorder.

Below is a list of helpful definitions that define signs, symptoms, and indicators. Typical signs of mental illness identifying the difference between typical behaviors and signs can be challenging.

It is often difficult to recognize the early warning signs that may indicate the onset of mental illness. According to Mental Health America, it is especially important to pay attention to sudden changes in thoughts and behaviors.

When a combination of these changes occurs at the same time, it may indicate a problem that should be addressed. The symptoms below should not be due to recent substance abuse or other medical conditions. Mental Health America identifies these signs in children, adolescents, and adults:

- Confused thinking
- Prolonged depression (sadness or irritability)
- Feelings of extreme highs and lows
- Excessive fears, worry, and anxieties
- Social withdrawal
- Dramatic changes in eating or sleeping habits
- Strong feelings of anger often related to domestic violence
- Strange thoughts (delusions)
- Seeing or hearing things that aren't there (hallucinations)
- Growing inability to cope with daily problems and activities
- Suicidal thoughts
- Numerous unexplained physical ailments
- Substance abuse

As with other health conditions, mental illnesses are often physical as well as emotional and psychological. They may be caused by a reaction to environmental stresses, genetic factors, biochemical imbalances, or a combination of these. With proper care and treatment, many people learn to cope with their illness and continue functioning in their daily lives. Mental illness is real and highly treatable. Here is a list of terms and definitions that can be helpful in identifying what mental health behavior can be like:

### Anxiety Disorders

People with anxiety disorders respond to certain objects or situations with fear and dread. Anxiety disorders can include obsessive-compulsive disorder, panic disorders, and phobias.

### Behavioral Disorders

Behavioral disorders involve a pattern of disruptive behaviors in children that last for at least six months and cause problems in school, at home, and in social situations. Examples of behavioral disorders include attention deficit hyperactive disorder (ADHD), conduct disorder, and oppositional-defiant disorder (ODD).

### Eating Disorders

Eating disorders involve extreme emotions, attitudes, and behaviors involving weight and food. They can include anorexia, bulimia, and binge eating.

### Mental Health and Substance Use Disorders

Mental health problems and substance abuse disorders sometimes occur together.

### Mood Disorders

Mood disorders involve persistent feelings of sadness or periods of feeling overly happy or fluctuating between extreme happiness and extreme sadness. Mood disorders can include depression, bipolar disorder, seasonal affective disorder (SAD), and self-harm.

### Obsessive-Compulsive Disorder

If you have OCD, you have repeated, upsetting thoughts called obsessions. You do the same thing repeatedly to try to make the thoughts go away. Those repeated actions are called compulsions.

### Personality Disorders

People with personality disorders have extreme, inflexible, distressing personality traits that may cause problems at work, school, or in social relationships. Personality disorders can include antisocial personality disorder and borderline personality disorder.

### Psychotic Disorders

People with psychotic disorders experience a range of symptoms, including hallucinations and delusions. An example of a psychotic disorder is schizophrenia.

### Suicidal Behavior

Suicide causes immeasurable pain, suffering, and loss to individuals, families, and communities nationwide.

### Trauma and Stress-Related Disorders

Post-traumatic stress disorder (PTSD) can occur after living through or seeing a traumatic event, such as war, a hurricane, rape, physical abuse, or a bad accident. PTSD makes you feel stressed and afraid after the danger is over.

These are the people who are quiet and may isolate themselves at church and gradually be missing in service. They often feel they won't be missed at church, their prayers are unanswered, and that spiritual things don't apply to them. They are wandering spirits that have not been given an assignment in worship or normal church activities as a part of the inclusion of church life in general. They feel that no one cares.

Congregants often told me, "We have some bad children in our church." This is not a good thing to hear. The pastoral care unit must fully understand that some children may have attention deficit disorder, which can masquerade as behavior problems such as impulsive behavior, hyperactivity, and an inability to focus on non-interesting topics. This can take place at church and at school and should be observed at the playground.

A valuable lesson around mental health behavior can be learned by observation of daily activities. We can gain a sense of direction that will determine how to support those who need our understanding and care.

We must learn what problems look like and become educated in becoming the health care church. Every church needs a mental health plan in place. Below are a few suggestions for creating a mental health plan within your local church or reconstructing your existing wellness plan to be more inclusive in its outreach mission.

We all learn one from another and understand that some things work better in different churches as the need demands. Here are a few questions that all can consider as we develop a helpful plan that supports those who are suffering emotional or mental illness within our churches and beyond:

• How can the church be more proactive in the way it offers inclusion and provides an accepting fellowship and kind spirit for people with mental health problems?

- What resources within our church can we offer to people experiencing mental health problems?
- How can church people reduce the potential damage and stigma that religion might bring about in people who are vulnerable?
- How can the ministry of the local church and professional helps complement the healing associated with church therapies, professional care, or taking medication as well as the support of friends, family, and other users of mental health services?

We must have an honest and open dialogue about our common spiritual needs. What are they, and how do we meet our own? How do they relate to mental health? How do we make sure they are not neglected? How can we as Christians provide the love, support, and understanding that people with mental health problems turn to us for? If we were honest with ourselves, we would ask ourselves what's wrong with us. People with mental health issues may not sing in tune but want to worship God. How can the church respond?

Below is some material resource information from LifeWay and other health care providers we have found helpful here at God's Way.

1. Identify strategies to enhance clergy, congregants, and the African American community's awareness about mental health and recovery. Here is a list of things the local church can do to develop a safe, loving, and caring mental health program that respects everyone. These ideas are only focal points for discussion in developing a mental health program unique to your church.

- Provide a forum for people involved in pastoral care to share issues related to work with people who are mentally unwell
- Explore the relationship between spirituality and mental health and identify specific ways in which the church can support people in distress or their emotional well being
- Look at ways of providing support to vulnerable people
- Share experiences and difficulties faced in pastoral work and think about the areas where more guidance and support are needed
- Consider what constitutes a mental disturbance. When are experiences valid manifestations of spirituality? How can we help people struggling with these issues?
- Evaluate how can we recognize and remember that there is more to the person than their illness thinks about everything the person has to offer
- What specific support can the church offer?

There must be a mental health focus within the local church: Is it safe to be honest here? Will I face rejection and blame? Will I be abandoned? Will I just be preached at and talked about? Will I be stared at? Will anyone walk beside me during my struggles? Will I find forgiveness and redemption in this place? Will I be treated with the same respect and dignity? Will I be allowed to be a part of the worship experience at my church? These are broad questions that are raised around mental health. Think about the things listed below for a moment. Remember our mission is to eliminate the stigma. We don't need to react—we need to respond.

- Think about the needs of different people with mental health problems and how to respond sensitively to their situations
- Develop an action plan for setting up support within the church community

- Raise awareness of the needs of mental wellness within the church community affected by mental illness health
- Explore ways in which the church can offer support to people caring for family with mental health issues
- Think about the difficulties that the mentally ill may face
- Consider how the church can ensure issues around confidentiality and boundaries are established
- Evaluate what kind of support could be developed for emotional wellness
- Increase understanding and awareness about mental health issues
- Provide an opportunity for volunteers to develop listening and interpersonal skills and ways to cope with emotional distress
- Create a safe environment and learn to listen as a part of inclusion
- Set up an ongoing support system for volunteers
- Create a welcoming atmosphere and involve participants as much as possible in the running of the scheme. Determine how to get the right ethos and avoid an us vs. them approach
- Consider ground rules that will be needed and how to negotiate them with the group participants[1]
- Think about how you can provide support to the volunteers – volunteers need to know who to turn to when they need support between group meetings
- Discuss how to befriend, make connections, see potential in others, and honor the humanity of all those with whom we share our life and come into contact
- Learn to listen to our own inner voice(s), to the Spirit of God, to what others are really saying

2.  Strategies for partnering with local provider agencies and clinicians, both in the church and faith-based community, to identify culturally appropriate resources for congregants and those beyond. There is no danger in the church partnering with outside counselors and professional helps.

Those from black and minority ethnic communities with mental health problems face barriers to accessing mental health services. For some people, faith communities may be the first point of contact and can act as a link and referral system to statutory mental health services and other sources of support in the community.

Faith communities can play a key role in forging partnerships with mental health service providers and supporting people to seek professional help. The African American Family Support Conference is a powerful tool that offers support, education, and recourses that can be helpful and informative for the mental health initiative.

You will need a support group, know who your team is, and develop a strong and lasting relationship with each team player. The team that supports your mental health program should consist of the fire department, police, sheriff, social worker, health advocate, hospital administrators, pastors, and professional helps. Build your base by connecting with other faith-based initiatives of like concerns.

A spiritual forum and partnership support should team up as a mental health integrity assistance program, a total wrap-around service. Below I have mentioned two distinct kinds of support groups.

## Spiritual Support

A network provides an opportunity for people from mental health, from faith-based communities, and for people who use mental health services to meet, debate relevant issues and exchange ideas, educate, update, discuss coming events, explore resources, and create opportunities for a dialogue with those who need to understand the different cultures and religious backgrounds and its impact upon those suffering mental illness.

Spiritual leaders and the professional world can better work together to create a total care package supporting tool that provides the necessary help needed.

## Partnership Support

The church is already actively involved in many local partnerships and can play an important part, for example, in working to support local groups within church communities to play a significant role in turning their neighborhoods around and help create a stigma-free environment. The church must have a voice at the table.

God's Way offers a wellness empowerment community ministry, WECM, as a support program. We are now partnering with local churches, Nami, Life Steps, Bluebonnet, Wilco, and Pavilion Care. All are effective players and offer an opportunity to support our work on inclusive mental health equality and spirituality.

There are many potential benefits of increasing partnership between statutory, voluntary, community services and faith-based communities to provide support for people with mental health problems. In the quest for mental health team support, there are both spiritual and cultural significances.

The spiritual dimension has a significant importance in many people's lives. People working within primary care, specialists, mental health services, or other organizations provide support and care for people with mental health problems.

We must be aware of the importance of religious and spiritual beliefs for many people as part of their support and recovery process. Therefore, mental health support must be looked at as a team concept. Those who have mental problems are offered a package deal as part of the healing process, conducive to their belief.

Faith-based communities have a key role in promoting this increased awareness and understanding, to ensure that services are sensitive to people's needs and not interpret religious expression as a symptom of illness.

Developing partnerships and mutual respect between faith-based communities and health professionals can help increase awareness, with mental health service providers and survivor groups also having an important contribution to make.

Advocacy services can help ensure that service providers, especially those from black and minority ethnic communities, have their views known and their cultural and religious beliefs respected. This may be important if people's religious beliefs, lifestyle choices, and expressions of their cultural identity are not to be interpreted as part of their psychiatric diagnosis.

Focusing on what is happening, what identity looks like and recognizing spiritual beliefs helps us recognize our common humanity and the essential solidarity between mental health service providers, pastors, caretakers, and staff members.

# CHAPTER THREE

# THE NEED FOR SPIRITUAL DISCERNMENT

*L*et's take another look through the spiritual lens, and we might discover that we can no longer view mental illness as amoral or the aspects of a spiritual failure syndrome. Let's see if a biochemical condition is occurring. There should be an appropriate response to the demands of mental health, as previously mentioned. There should be a unique perspective on how we perceive the human behavior around us. Sometimes we just need to look a little closer, listen a little more, and reach out a little further.

There may be difficulties in balancing both the spiritual and physical needs of those who are suffering mental illness, in addition to poor judgment or oversight, member evaluation discrepancy, neglect because of a lack of knowledge, and proper assessment.

We must think about what's right for everyone, what's needed for everyone, and whether everyone is included, supported, loved, and cared for as an integral part of that local ministry, which connects the spiritual, mental, and physical aspects of life as wholeness, wellness, and fulfillment.

There must be an honest dialogue among congregants concerning mental illness and its symptoms and causes in the same manner we would with any other type of illness.

We must develop the ability to discern, sense, feel, and develop a mindset that understands the need of those suffering within our realm of support, the need to increase in knowledge, and the need for continuing to learn about mental health issues. We are a work in progress. I have visited many pastors and noted that small churches may have one person, but most of the pastoral staff is not trained to treat mental illness or offer counseling services. Most megachurches have professional counselors on staff, and they are to be commended for their services.

There is no excuse for not having mental health awareness programs, workshops, and sermons that encourage and inform congregants that they can turn to church leaders and be directed to our partners providing professional helps and those working in faith-based communities. We are stronger together. Proverbs 18:14 says the human spirit will endure sickness, but a broken spirit who can bear?

We are not here to hurt or harm; we are here to help. If the spirit is wounded and hurting, it does not matter how healthy or strong your body might be. You must never allow a condition to have victory over your spirit. The Bible indeed recognizes the very depths that psychological pain can reach. We all have had our share of life's ups and downs and unexpected trauma, some self-inflicted at times, by those who do not care.

Spiritual sensory is being aware of God's presence in the present moment, right where we are. An effective way to cultivate this mindfulness is to pay attention to the five senses—they serve as good relationship builders. Let's look at them as spiritual tools that God has equipped us with to do ministry.

God speaks to us through what we see, hear, smell, touch, and taste. We know this intuitively but thinking about it consciously is a powerful form of prayer and service. We're experiencing the creative goodness of God. We can and should find God in all things and, most of all, in people. We must connect with people and their needs.

God meets us where we are, as humans living, breathing, and moving in a tangible world, and the five senses are five entry points for God's love to become known to us. We all have a God-given ability to see, hear, touch, and discern the need to help all people regardless of who they are, where they live, or their mental or physical conditions.

It's up to us to learn about mental health and the ways we can support it. There are those suffering mental illness while serving as pastors and church leaders and among lay membership, and they need support.

Numerous Bible characters endured mental illness while being called of God; they served while depressed. Consider Elijah's story (1 Kings 19), Hannah's story (1 Samuel 1), the apostle Paul's thorn (2 Corinthians 12), and King David in the book of Psalms.

Mental health has always been a ministry need within the local church realm of hope. Yet another type of stigma is denial and not admitting that we struggle with depression or some type of emotional or mental illness. We are ashamed or embarrassed and not willing to verbalize that we are suffering in silence. We believe we will be recognized as one who has a character flaw, one of weak faith, even problematic to some.

So how can we normalize mental health among our congregants? We must talk about these struggles that are real in each of our lives—we all know somebody. No one should be ashamed or embarrassed to share their stories. We should just see them as elements of our human condition that we all face daily. We all have limited abilities. Spiritually, we all have been instructed to depend upon the ability that God has given each of us to use in this life that is designed to profit all (Ephesians 3:20-21).

People involved in providing spiritual and pastoral care may benefit from information and training from mental health specialists to help them understand issues around mental health and illness, identify ways they can help, and recognize their limitations and boundaries.

This can enable faith-based communities to better include and support people coping with the effects of mental distress and mental health in their community and support people in a way which promotes positive mental health and assists in recovery.

When planning and delivering training on mental health promotion within your local church community, it can be helpful to involve the expertise of a local mental health professional, for example, a community psychiatric nurse, clinical director, psychologist, or someone working in a local mental health voluntary agency. The police and fire departments should also be a part of that support team, for they are often first responders. Pastors are also classified as first responders as well.

How can we address mental health in our place of worship? These specific strategies may be helpful as we engage in mental health discussions concerning emotional wellness and recovery. How do we address mental health, what are they, how can we meet our own needs as well as others, and how can we be sure they are not neglected? What kind of quality care do our congregants have one for another? Can they become part of a community effort to normalize mental health and take away the stigma that has plagued so many?

Church therapy may not be a practical idea among many congregants, nor the idea of having a therapy session at church. I believe church therapy will bring about humanization among congregants that is all pleasing to God. This will undo the harm being perpetrated by stigma-related issues that don't constitute a perfect marriage or union at church. It is the providential will and work of God that there be a one-God-centered family.

As a pastor, I have seen firsthand that those struggling with mental health problems are neglected and mentally harmed by those who profess to know Christ. Some of our actions are a little pharisaical at church.

Church therapy among congregants can be most helpful because it offers a degree of mental awareness to everyone and develops team inclusion concepts and unifying and team-building techniques. Proverbs 11:14 says a nation falls through lack of guidance, but victory comes through the counsel of many. Let's consider Ephesians 4:22-24 and be renewed in the spirit of our mind. We all have room for improvement.

I believe the church is responsible for educating all congregants. Now, more than ever, it is vital that we address the whole person, their social and emotional well-being, which can occur through a church therapy session. Through church therapy, we learn how to feel about ourselves and how others will react to our feelings, how to think about these feelings and what choices we have in reacting, and how to read and express hopes and fears.

Social and emotional development is a process which allows congregants to acquire and effectively apply the knowledge, attitudes, and skills necessary to understand and manage their emotions, set and achieve positive goals, feel and show empathy for others, establish and maintain positive relationships, and make responsible decisions.

Social and emotional awareness is a powerful way to help congregants see the person, not the illness, and become healthy, caring, and competent.

I believe when congregants learn to express emotions constructively and engage in caring and respectful relationships in the beginning stages, they give birth to a compassionate spirit. The end results are that inclusion is born and the stigma ends.

Within the daily operations of church ministries, a model mental health safety plan should be put in place for all church leaders and congregants. Below is a list of concepts that will enhance member participation as a part of inclusion and diversity within the local church.

As discussed, church therapy has to do mostly with disciplinary practices, member diversity, and culture exchange—the ability to share your spirit with another, share moments of hope, and mentor one to another. It is the usage of words, feelings, social engagement, emotions, relationships, problems, expressions, etc. in their proper settings. This gives birth to a genuine dialogue that leads to a deep connection of trust, such as sharing a special one-on-one moment or a thought, which can be so significant in that special moment of need.

Realistically speaking, what does a safe place look like at church? Is there a talk space, ministry space, or even a social space? Is there a time we might need a little me space as well? Every congregant seeks that at times because we all have our moments of disparities and human concerns.

The church is supposed to create an excellent atmosphere, a better day, working relationships, and new beginnings for all of God's children. There a Silent church trauma should never be provoked. Not everyone who attends church will have the compassion and interest of others at heart.

So many times, we get caught up in our own auxiliaries, activities, family, and needs that we forget the main purpose we serve—simply to help people. Many questions about where we are and what we do needs answers to address a church problem or mental health issue. As I mentioned earlier, good behavior concepts should be put in place as a regulatory compliance guide within our local church and beyond that everyone adheres to. I believe mental health briefing should be part of the new member orientation.

- Is our church a safe place for everyone? Do our environment and atmosphere send a clear message of welcome to everyone, and are we supportive of their personal needs?

- Do we offer support, patience, and compassion to everyone? How can we offer support to those serving in ministry who may be ashamed or embarrassed to ask for help from their local church while serving as pastor or others serving within ministry?
- It is a challenge to work with and walk alongside one with mental illness to the place where help is available, the place where the need is completely met.
- How can those with mental illness challenges participate in worship and have an active role in ministry?
- How can we understand and communicate proper language about mental health? How can we recognize spiritual support and professional support and how they work together for mental recovery?
- How can the individuality and uniqueness of each person's spirituality be recognized, respected, and responded to with care and genuine love?
- How can people working in mental health services be enabled to talk to service users about spiritual and religious needs, both when they first get assessed and throughout their care and treatment?
- How can mental health services be helped to offer access to religious and spiritual resources, including people trained and knowledgeable about spiritual issues and opportunities for groups to discuss these issues?

How can effective networks be built between different faith-based communities and mental health services locally and nationally? Natisha

Stewart, counselor at the Potter House Dallas, Texas, gave me a key concept: just start where you are.

How true those words were. Within our reach were numerous organizations just waiting to help us become successful in our wellness program. Professionals volunteered and served as our voice to other faith-based initiatives that were unknown to us. They are now part of our networking around mental and emotional well-being.

# CHAPTER FOUR

# WHAT WE NEED TO KNOW
# AT CHURCH

*M*any blacks and minority groups across Americans from all walks of life don't get help, either because they fear both spiritual and secular stigma or they simply cannot afford treatment and do not know where resources are.

Mental illness as it relates to church folks can often be overlooked and misunderstood in the struggles of life because of a lack of knowledge and the inability to address such issues appropriately. The stigma will only cease to exist when people are valued for who they are. The voice of disparity is a human cry and must be heard within the local church and beyond to meet the demand of the underserved.

Mental health must be defined as a need like any other struggle. Look around you on any given Sunday. Most likely, Christians next to you are suffering silently from anxiety or panic disorder, bipolar disorder, dysthymia, or major depressive disorder.

Whether through personal experience or through someone we know, those of us whose lives have been touched by mental health struggles know that getting help can be the hardest part, which is a struggle within itself.

Even while at church, it is often difficult to be accepted and hard for people to understand that some days are difficult. Help is needed without discrimination and a true love without dissimulation. Scripture teaches that a friend is born for adversity, so you would think someone would always be there to help. In many cases, the support for mental health among those who need our attention for moral, physical, and mental support is often discouraged or pushed or shushed.

A story in Mark 10:46–52 helps us define what the church should do to help someone crying out for attention and support from others within their reach and ability. At Jericho's northern gate, a blind beggar named Bartimaeus sat at a well-established place. Day after day, the world passed by this blind man, rarely noticing him, certainly not caring about him. The blind man heard children laughing and playing around, some gossiping in the marketplace. He could hear men and women walking about traveling to their destinations for the day, but he saw nothing because he was confined by blindness.

In many ways, Bartimaeus was not thought of until that special day when Jesus passed his way. Sensing the excitement, Bartimaeus asked those around him what was happening, and they told him that Jesus of Nazareth, the great healer, the balm of Gilead, was passing through.

Bartimaeus knew he could not ignore this opportunity. We hear Jesus pose a question to a blind man: "What do you want me to do for you?" We must ask others the same question today as we are passing by. The question is, will you stop today to help?

Bartimaeus, the blind beggar at the side of the road, suffered the loss of his sight earlier in his life. We can imagine that this beggar was not very attractive. He would have been like many of the unwanted people we try to keep out of sight. But though his prospects were limited, his faith and optimistic spirit were strong.

When he heard Jesus was passing by, Bartimaeus was determined to grasp this opportunity. He ignored those who told him to be quiet, crying out to Jesus. When a soft voice did not work, he began to bellow: "Jesus, Son of David, have mercy on me!" Somehow this blind man reached out in hope toward a heavenly Radiance he could sense, even if he could not see, and those around him were non-supportive. "Jesus, Son of David, have mercy on me!"

Congregants are non-supportive and not willing to follow through in the process of mental health restoration. Those in our churches suffer with mental health problems even after having received professional help from doctors and therapy. Even then, the recovery process has been hindered by words spoken out of context, bad advice, jesters, mistreatment, and poor choices about who to rely on. It is devastating and not fair.

Unfortunately, many of us who have spoken up in church have been told to "pray harder" or "have more faith." These suggestions are often well-intentioned, but they discourage, hinder, and isolate those who desperately need our support. It is tear-jerking to judge people when they're vulnerable and exposing their conditions.

As people living in the Christian community, we should be ready to offer practical knowledge and gracious support to people experiencing mental health crises. Everyone needs a reason to keep trying and given the opportunity to live and let live. If someone in your church or community is suffering, come alongside them today. Pray for them. Avoid cheap platitudes like "have faith" and instead offer practical support by checking in regularly to let them know they are not alone. Ask about their treatment or health, which is a way of acknowledging that the illness is real and so are your concerns about their needs. There is always a need to pray; prayer is a vital part of the healing process.

It is reassuring to know that Christianity offers a promise of restoration greater than anything we can ever imagine. In the Bible, people often fall or come short in many situations, and the same is true of us today. The good news was that God raised them up again and again. He is the lifter of the weary soul, the God of our silent tears and weary years, the restorer of our failing health.

Much like spiritual and physical health, mental and emotional health is an ongoing need for every human being. Although those who struggle mentally are each responsible for themselves, they should be able to rely on the powerful support of their local church and community along with care providers to ensure that they get the care they need.

It all starts with awareness. Each local church must reach within to offer help and support. It is time for us to recognize that those who are struggling within our congregations and faith-based communities can live a normal and empowered life with mental illness. Christians must break the stigma and shame of mental illness. Yes, you can and yes, we will.

The Bible is filled with exhortations to care for the most vulnerable among us, those who cry out for mercy and feel they have nowhere to turn. Those of us who face mental health crises are among the most vulnerable. We need your recognition. We need your prayers. We need your presence. And we need to be part of the church community, especially as we struggle to find extra grace to live a better day.

Here are some very helpful verses from the KJV emphasizing God's strength, guidance, love, and provision for those who may feel depressed, hopeless, burned out, or stressed:

### Deuteronomy 31:8

And the Lord, he it is that doth go before thee; he will be with thee, he will not fail thee, neither forsake thee: fear not, neither be dismayed.

### Psalm 16:8

I have set the Lord always before me: because he is at my right hand, I shall not be moved.

### Psalm 56:3–4

What time I am afraid, I will trust in thee. In God I will praise his word, in God I have put my trust; I will not fear what flesh can do unto me.

### John 16:33

These things I have spoken unto you, that in me ye might have peace. In the world ye shall have tribulation: but be of good cheer; I have overcome the world.

### John 14:27

Peace I leave with you, my peace I give unto you: not as the world giveth, give I unto you. Let not your heart be troubled, neither let it be afraid.

### Philippians 4:6–7

Be careful for nothing; but in everything by prayer and supplication with thanksgiving let your requests be made known unto God. And the peace of God, which passeth all understanding, shall keep your hearts and minds through Christ Jesus.

### Psalm 32:7–8

Thou art my hiding place; thou shalt preserve me from trouble; thou shalt compass me about with songs of deliverance. Selah. I will instruct thee and teach thee in the way which thou shalt go: I will guide thee with mine eye.

### 2 Corinthians 11:27–28

In weariness and painfulness, in watchings often, in hunger and thirst, in fastings often, in cold and nakedness. Beside those things that are without, that which cometh upon me daily, the care of all the churches.

### Psalm 34:17

The righteous cry, and the Lord heareth, and delivereth them out of all their troubles.

# CHAPTER FIVE

# MENTAL HEALTH STORIES

*B*eing hands-on with mental health concerns can be challenging within our congregations. Listening and patience are powerful tools in conveying support among those we know and love. Mental health issues are real within our pews.

Our pastoral staff has demonstrated complete spiritual support and unconditional love to congregants about medications and professional helps. We learned that there can be competing narratives among congregants living with mental conditions.

We had to carefully listen to several family members without being judgmental. Not everyone had the best interest of the person at heart, and the person seeking compassion and support had a distinct perspective of what the need was. It's about assessing and ministering effectively to help those who need our help. Listening is one of the senses we need to develop in the church.

We were successful in bringing balance through spiritual guidance. One out of five sitting in our pews is suffering in silence. Mental health can be complicated and often difficult to deal with and, in many areas, sensitive. Mental health requires effective team support, love, understanding, and the ability to problem solve without being opinionated. The winning factors should be geared toward the one suffering from mental health issues. Their need is what matters.

Health and wellness are integral parts of a sustainable future, and it is essential for people to be healthy, both physically and mentally, to thrive. As opportunity presents itself, let us be mindful of the shared responsibility of helping everyone be the best they can be for the glory of God. God intentionally blessed everyone with a gift that can be valued and appreciated by others. We were designed to belong together, work together, play together, praise and worship together, and even live together as God's children. We are called to be a blessing one to another.

## Nicole Traphan

Ms. Nicole Traphan is a Christian who loves her church here at God's Way. She is multitalented and involved in several ministries and supportive to many while occupying a full-time job. She has challenges with her son. Her story is an encouragement to other parents and congregants and helpful in teaching other families with youth how to cope, understand their specific needs, and use their voices to get the assistance they need to be supported at school, in their homes, and in their church life. She shares her story—ADD or Not!

I embarked on a journey toward mental health with my son many years ago. When I think back, I always thought things seemed more difficult raising my youngest son than with my oldest son. I was forced to begin confronting his issues when he started school.

In kindergarten, he kicked his teacher, and the teacher had him permanently removed from her class. He went on to terrorize another teacher for the remainder of the year. I spanked him, and he told the staff at school. I was investigated by CPS, and it wouldn't be the only time CPS would visit my home due to complaints by the school.

It is a struggle as an African American parent to accept and/or pursue a diagnosis of attention deficit disorder for a child. On one hand, there is the issue of over-diagnosis, and on the other is the stigma associated with the diagnosis.

In the beginning, the primary consideration was development. Not all children develop at the same rates, particularly male children who historically have slower growth rates. I looked at the development from a longitudinal aspect, meaning I looked at his growth from infancy to see if I thought he was on track with his peers. He was slow to speak, and it was probably age three before he spoke sentences, stringing three or four words together. I also looked at him in a current view.

He routinely didn't turn in homework after we had worked on it together and I placed it in his backpack. He wasn't completing his work in class and would leave the classroom only to lose it. He wasn't just making bad grades—the grades were a symptom of something larger.

Most parents seek help in controlling their children's behavior. There is a misconception that behavior is the product of attitude or personality. Behavior is a product of brain function. Despite hundreds of years of research on human brain function, little is known about it.

The brain controls 100 percent of a human's daily activity. Over 80 percent of these brain processes occur involuntarily, meaning without conscious thought or decision-making.

Many brain disorders share the same symptoms. A mood disorder can affect a child's behavior, making him irritable and distracted. This translates to a child being more likely to engage in fights and being slow to complete school work. An executive functioning disorder can affect a child's behavior, making him seem defiant.

This translates to a child being more likely to fail to do assigned tasks and being off task and engaged in talking after several warnings. Both disorders have the same symptoms as attention deficit disorder. A neuropsychological evaluation provides different testing methods that help provide a clearer picture of what may be causing behavior issues.

After a neuropsychological evaluation, a doctor may advise medication for treatment of a disorder. It is important for parents to ask about side effects and weigh the costs versus the benefits for medications. Some children can improve with cognitive behavior therapy or occupational therapy.

These services can be accessed through the schools with a 504 education plan. Some drugs require medical supervision, including regular doctor's visits and blood tests. Consequently, children, with the right medication, have marked improvements in their grades and behavior. It is important to document when and if a child is improving and make changes when necessary.

My son's ADD is comorbid (occurring together) with depression. Before the neuropsychological evaluation, he was being treated with medication for his depression because he was routinely threatening to self-harm. The ADD and depression feed each other. My son doesn't do well in school, so he feels stupid. Other students teased and bullied him.

I began by stating that I was on a journey toward mental health. We haven't reached our destination, but I choose to believe we are still on the path. Ultimately, it is not a diagnosis that defines who a child is and it important for parents to do their best to ensure their children are healthy, productive, and successful.

## Rhonda's Bio

Rhonda Franklin-Romar, CPS, BSW, considers herself a "People Enthusiast." As a local and national inspirational and motivational speaker, she continues to support her own recovery journey through sharing her own lived experiences.

As a mental health advocate, Rhonda realized that many of us are broken and live silently, destroying ourselves and others physically and emotionally as we strive to cling to GOD's Word and stay connected to Him.

She shares her personal story, her struggles with mental health, and her battles within the church walls and beyond. She is an encouragement to many that there is a way through to a victorious life.

Her story is remarkable as she speaks about how her defeats turned to triumph on her health journey to victorious living while experiencing her personal mental health concerns. She claims Christ as the lifter of her soul.

Rhonda's recovery from a mental health crisis began years ago. Along with therapy, she started to share her lived experiences. Her long-time friend gave her the opportunity to share her story locally at The A.R. Hargrove Family Life Center. Later, she began speaking at the well-known Central Texas African American Family Support Conference, ACC Women's Health, Motivation, and Empowerment conferences.

She has been a panelist speaker for several venues, including The Way to Wellness conference presented by God's Way Christian Baptist Church. Rhonda is a certified peer specialist and was blessed to speak before the Travis County Commissioners Court as she and others accepted the resolution, proclaiming May 3, 2015 as "National Mental Health and Dignity Day" in Travis County. Rhonda has traveled nationally to present/co-present at Alternative's 2017 and WRAP Around the World.

Rhonda has been equipped with a unique compassion for her audiences and is as passionate about the topics she presents, such as "They Took My Wonder Women Card: How to be Perfectly Imperfect," "It Really is OK!!," "A Day in the Life of Mental Health Recovery," "Resiliency: Coming Through a Storm," and one of her favorites, "Broken Mosaic," just to name a few.

She certainly expresses all honor, praise, and thanks to her Lord and Savior, Jesus Christ—the one who saved her and has given her a pathway to peace, understanding, love, and grace. "The Lord is merciful and gracious, slow to anger, and plenteous in mercy" (Psalm 103:8 KJV).

Rhonda shares her story:

My belief and hope is that my lived experiences are more relevant than my accolades and education. My lived experiences include living with several mental health diagnoses. My lived experiences have strengthened my faith, encouraged me, taught me how to be empathetic and compassionate to others, and set me on a path of learning more about myself and helping others by sharing my story. I hope that this will be one of your takeaways from my contribution to this blessed manuscript.

While growing up and into adulthood, I cannot recall ever hearing words like "mental health," "mental health diagnosis," "mental illness," or "mental wellness." I did, however, know something was not right, or should I say something was "off" with my mood, behavior, retention of information, or lack thereof, the continuous thoughts of suicide, hiding out (isolation), low self-esteem, and the list goes on. I did not realize the extent of my troubles, symptoms, and obstacles—at least, not until after I married and had children. I always felt like I was wrapped differently than most of the people I interacted with. I did not need a rocket scientist, therapist, or counselor to tell me "if" there was something wrong; instead, I wanted to know the "what, why, and how to fix it."

While I was growing up, I always wondered why no one in church noticed that something was not right with our family. Why didn't anyone see the sadness in my eyes, behind my beautiful face and smile? Why didn't anyone see that I was a bit jumpy and slothful with each task given? Why didn't anyone ask the right questions? Do you feel safe? Do you ever have thoughts of suicide? But no one did. There was no one to share my secret with. Who would believe me?

During my youth, the church's youth department and youth choir were safe outlets to avoid being home. I was able to go on youth trips. This was so exciting. I love being outside and having fun. No one knew, or at least appeared to not know, about the trauma I was experiencing at home.

I guess it was impossible for the church to be supportive. Church folks back then didn't have a dictionary or vocabulary to express what myself and many other adults and kids were experiencing. No one around me used words like anxiety or depression or talked about symptoms. I would, however, hear words like, "There's nothing wrong with you." People thought someone getting a whooping would make it all better. It didn't though. It made my trauma worse.

As I grew into an adult, I could no longer avoid and deny; something that wasn't good continued to happen to me. I picked up learned behaviors that needed to change for my generation. I now had four people relying on me to live a better life, i.e., away from chaotic behaviors of anger, rage, sadness, extreme loneliness, mood swings, flashbacks of traumatic events, isolation, etc. I realized early on these four people that were irrefutably counting on me were my three young children and myself. Sadly, I wished I could have figured it all out before kids, before a failed marriage, before attending college the first time, or before I turned 20 and moved away from home.

Although I have been in church most of my life, I had never shared my mental health disorders with anyone in that arena. As an adult, I found my therapy was to share my story with strangers for their healing and mine.

On the other hand (another important take away), *when you do not have a safe place, people will most often shut down, resulting in a missed opportunity for healing.* This sometimes happens when people are judgmental. When they think they know more about you than you know about yourself. In group, we were taught to keep our thoughts focused on ourselves, not on others (those who hurt us). This was the best gift at the time I could give to myself. If I kept my thoughts focused on others and their actions, I would miss out on all the lessons I desired for my healing. I'd like to share a few of the lessons with you, that I have learned along the way through my mental health journey. Right or Wrong; Good or Bad

I believe too often we insert our perspective onto others and what we think they should do about their struggles. I love the example that Jesus left for us. When religious leaders and the public wanted to cast stones and judge the promiscuous woman, Jesus provided an opportunity for those with opinions to be the first to cast stones. No one could. The lesson for us may be to focus more on our own problems and issues as we seek ways to transform our lives for the better. Whether we think someone is doing right or wrong, good or bad, often it comes down to one's own perspective.

Perspective means each person has their own viewpoint. I'm not talking about the commandments or laws of the Bible. Take a moment and think...If our neighbor is not intentionally or willfully hurting us or others, unless they ask for help or want help, we should tread lightly with a heavy dose of love and the desire to "understand and be understood," as my mother-in-law would say.

### Activating My Triggers

In my recovery journey, I wanted to understand more about the people, places, and things that would activate my triggers. I realized over the years that these same triggers continued to create obstacles for me. I felt stuck and thought I would not get better. I realized some things I had personal control over and other things, I did not. Have you ever thought about the effects of the things you may say or do that could **cause a person to be more anxious than usual**? Things that may **amplify a person's illness**? If you haven't, now's your time to do so. I will share a few stories with you: "Train your Neck" and "Blessings and Cursings."

### Train Your Neck

Have you ever been in the middle of Sunday worship service and someone new walks in? If you've been there, this is the time that people would stop paying attention to the preacher and the word being preached and turn around to see who was walking into the church. Church members would stop, turn, and stare for what felt like a lifetime. Maybe you feel it's normal or it's a habit. Well, this may be true. I'm asking you to think past what we call normal and think for just a moment... Read on...

What could activate a person's triggers for the person walking in? What about the women with three kids walking in church? Women of the church whisper in judgment, "She has too many kids." I do think about those things; are you willing to think about them too? I think we could all stand to "Train our neck." We can choose not to draw attention to people out of respect—you never know what issues they are going through. Staring and judgment have never helped anyone with a mood disorder, not that I am aware of. Come to think of it, if a man with three kids walked in, we would instead smile and ask if we could help. We'd be all too happy to. Hmmmm...

### *Blessings and Cursings*

Another example of activating a person's triggers that comes to mind is blessings and cursings. Do you suppose that saying something pleasant and then unkind to someone would help reduce or activate and increase their anxiety? How about shouting and cursing and belittling? This does not help reduce anxiety either. In fact, these actions can exasperate a person's condition more. Rather than getting irate with our loved ones, friends, and family who may be living with a mental illness or in recovery, we can often choose to forgive rather than traumatizing the issues. Believe it or not, grace and forgiveness help me with my symptoms.

This is not to simplify a person's mental illness, yet it could reduce the symptoms. I choose to forgive others so that those thoughts could not hold me captive at night and ruminate for hours—hours I'd rather spend sleeping. I must be honest—at times, my own behavior caused my symptoms to worsen, behaviors like anger, holding grudges, not being able to say no, and dealing with low self-esteem. Can you imagine that even eating the wrong foods with red dye or too much sugar or not eating at all is also a negative factor?

Believe it or not, I had to recognize that even social media was a harmful activating stimulate as well as a lack of sleep. I also found out I am allergic to drama, fussing, fighting, and arguing. Eventually, I no longer allowed my triggers and inevitably symptoms to hold me captive as much as I used to. I used the grace that God gave me and applied more of it to myself and others to get through, on the days when I choose not to make good choices.

### Grace and Mercy
Grace and mercy helped me deal with my disorders and the obstacles that each symptom created for me. God's grace and mercy taught me how to love myself and others even when I was not well. I look at God's grace as Him showing favor in my life in every way. If He loves me enough to forgive me of all my sins, symptoms, and shortcomings, I must be willing to do so for others. I smile when I think of his grace. I now know why I should love myself and others even during my downtime. Love kept the light on in my life during my dark times.

### Looking Back

When I look back on my life, I've been challenged with obstacles such as being comfortable in my own skin, knowing what my worth is, wondering what gift God gave me, and who really loves me. I've dealt with problematic friendships, partnerships, and the difficulty of trying to figure out who I am and where I belong. I have always felt that I was different, and not in a positive way. Having children and dealing with a divorce was the beginning of my self-realization. I have lived with anxiety, depression, ADHD, and their symptoms and not to mention my personal characteristics. I realized that if I am uncomfortable with who I am, then those around me may be as uncomfortable.

After years of healing, I realized that we are all different. God designed me exactly the way He planned. I was not a mistake or "different" in a negative way. It was through my imperfections and the journey of my healing that I became refined. Because of my healing, I am better equipped to relate to others, to also help them seek healing, to be an advocate for those who share my mental illness disorders. I would not be the person I am today without those struggles, without the journey to overcome. I still have ongoing struggles, as we all do, but I know the triggers that can set me off and I can better control my responses and not succumb to reactions. I am stronger and know from whom my strength comes.

Thank you for being a part of healing. Hopefully, you have learned what you can do better to help yourself and others. I pray that you will not only use this information but happily pass it along as an encouragement to someone who may be experiencing the same journey that so many of us have traveled.

God Bless.

## Eugenia Kleinpeter
### *The Rural Church Creating Inclusion Through Education*
by Josephine Gurch | Jun 11, 2018 | Hogg Blog |[1]

For more than 12 years, it was an uphill struggle for Eugenia Kleinpeter to locate mental health services for her children. Her eldest son, Greg—like four of his younger siblings—has special needs and spent time in the foster care system.

Like many in the African American community, and particularly in rural areas, Eugenia is actively involved in her church as an assistant minister and Sunday School teacher. Her church, God's Way Christian Baptist Church, is one of 11 faith-based organizations in African American communities that received funding through the Hogg Foundation's Faith-Based Initiative for African American Mental Health Education.

The initiative aims to capitalize on the unique role that churches and other faith-based organizations play in African American communities, and to use these organizations as conduits for mental health education and awareness. First launched in 2014 with $947,000 in grants distributed over three years, in 2017, the foundation added an additional year of funding, totaling $350,000, with a new focus on addressing the mental health impacts of Hurricane Harvey and other disasters.[2]

### *The Rural Church: A New Role to Play*
God's Way is based in Taylor, Texas and is led by Reverend Dr. B.R. Reese. The church used its grant funds to create a program called Wellness

and Empowerment Community Ministries (WECM), which offers church members a range of programs that help address psychological and spiritual needs.

For Eugenia Kleinpeter, God's Way's investment in mental health is paying dividends for her son Greg. Youth-oriented activities—pizza parties, bowling nights, and other fun-filled diversions—are combined with mental health education and guidance. "They don't stigmatize people there," she said. "God's Way truly embraced my children and encouraged them to use their talents."

The God's Way approach mirrors that of the other faith-based grantees. What they each have in common is years of involvement and earned credibility in the eyes of the people they serve, an ability to serve as a connector between congregants and available mental health services, and a willingness to innovate new programs and approaches where they don't currently exist.

For faith leaders and faith communities, involvement with the foundation is mutually beneficially. They are making strides in their ability to support individuals who have mental health needs, and openly acknowledge that certain traditional responses, such as the advice to "just pray it away," spread misconceptions around mental health and further stigmatize those who need adequate mental health services and supports.

### *Inclusion in Faith Circles through Mental Health Education*

African Americans are 20 percent more likely to experience serious mental health problems than non-Hispanic whites, according to the Office of Minority Health.

Even though the proportion of African Americans living with mental health conditions is not totally comparable with that of the general population, the National Alliance on Mental Illness reports that African

Americans consistently receive lower-quality and culturally incompetent mental health care.[3] This contributes to the greater severity of mental health issues among African Americans compared to non-Hispanic whites. Thus, African Americans frequently turn to spiritual advisors and circles to fill the gap.

### God's Way Christian Baptist Church

Led by Reverend Dr. B.R. Reese, God's Way Christian Baptist Church is one of 11 faith-based organizations that received funding through the Hogg Foundation's Faith-Based Initiative for African American Mental Health Education, which aims to build on the unique strengths of churches and faith-based organizations in African-American communities to increase awareness about and change perceptions of mental health, recovery and wellness, and to connect congregants with culturally competent behavioral health resources. Grantees have used the funds to start or strengthen dialogues about mental health—both within their respective places of worship and with providers in surrounding communities.

WECM provides a welcoming and inclusive space for congregants to engage in dialogue around mental health and has created a positive ripple effect, enhancing overall community well-being.

For more than 12 years, Eugenia Kleinpeter endured an uphill climb as she attempted to locate mental health services for her children. It's a struggle African Americans living in rural Texas know all too well. Eugenia's eldest son Greg, like four of his younger siblings, has special needs. As a child, he not only lacked adequate assistance for his speech impediment but also had to endure stigma from strangers and peers—even fellow churchgoers. "At church, my kids basically hung around me," said Eugenia. "There was a lot of rejection—a lot of people keeping their kids close to them, or not saying hello."

Often, in lieu of clinical sources of aid, African Americans turn to spiritual advisors and circles instead. At God's Way Christian Baptist Church, however, Eugenia and her son found both.

"They don't stigmatize people there. God's Way truly embraced my children and encouraged them to use their talents."

## *Mental Health Dialogues: From Pulpit to Barbershop*

When Greg was a teenager, Eugenia brought him to God's Way for the first time. "My son loves to go to church," she said. "He lights up when he sees the pastor. They've always included him—telling him they missed him and asking how he's been."

The church and its pioneering WECM initiatives have created a culture of inclusivity and sensitivity that provides for the congregation's spiritual and psychological needs. Though of modest size—the church convenes 50 to 100 attendees every Sunday—lessons learned and taught by God's Way clergy have, thanks to the evidence of success and word of mouth, traveled far and wide.

Health fairs, conferences, vacation Bible school programs, and other community awareness events are helmed by the leaders at God's Way—whose passion for mental health education, like Eugenia's, often stems from their own experiences of enlightenment.

Sonya Hosey, the church's associate pastor and project director of WECM, recalled the experience of growing up with a war veteran father who suffered from post-traumatic stress disorder (PTSD). "I never had answers as a child—there was never a name for it," she said. "Only as I began to work in the area of mental health did I finally understand some of the things he was going through."

That sense of understanding is what WECM education efforts try to impart to participants. With the help of partnerships with Bluebonnet

Trails Community Services, social service agencies, and other churches in Central Texas, Sonya organizes outreach events to share the critical mental health knowledge that is so beautifully helping God's Way congregants with other community members and leaders.

One of WECM's most successful programs is a series of barbershop dialogues, wherein representatives from God's Way and local law enforcement chat with barbershop patrons about the mental health issues afflicting the criminal justice system. The initiative is informed by Pastor Reese's belief in the need for first responders—pastors included—to come together and familiarize themselves with the unique nature of mental health emergencies. "We can educate them," he said. "We can let them know how to talk to someone with mental illness, instead of handcuffing or tazing them."

"I see us as a connector. We really look at the gaps and explore ones that some entities might not even be aware of."

### *Mental Health Education: Supporting Youth, Ending Stigma*

Greg's story sheds light on the importance of another principle of mental health education at God's Way: its focus on the youth. As a Sunday School teacher, Eugenia can attest to the enthusiasm her students show when learning about topics that typically don't see the light of day in public school curricula. "They're really inquisitive, and that helps us out," said Eugenia. "Because if we can help them, they'll help somebody else."

Youth-oriented activities mix entertainment—in the form of pizza parties, bowling nights, and other fun-filled diversions—with mental health education and guidance. Attendees even bring along friends. At these events, Sonya said, "They begin to understand signs and symptoms shown by their peers. And for them to ask so many questions—that's significant."

The dependable flood of questions is not just a sign of curiosity. It indicates that WECM educators have succeeded in fostering a quality of acceptance around subjects that might otherwise be misunderstood or stigmatized. "In our church, there are a lot of young people who live below the poverty line, or in single-parent households," said Pastor Reese. "Because they might not have all the resources they need, we have to run programs that will help them feel better about themselves—help them build self-esteem."

It's difficult to overstate just how valuable that can be for kids who are merely grappling with the normal emotions of coming of age, and more so for those experiencing stress and anxiety—or worse, trauma. "They're really trying to find out who they are, and it's more confusing now than when I was growing up," said Sonya. "We have to give them a voice. We have to listen."

### *The Ripple Effect: A Community That Supports Well-Being*

The faith-based initiative is part of the foundation's larger effort to build upon existing community strengths to enhance overall well-being. It also leverages the evidence base we have about how to do more than just infuse dollars, but to foster relationships that live beyond the grant term.

Despite the church's modest size, positive word of mouth about the accomplishments of Pastor Reese and God's Way has traveled far and wide, catching the attention of pastors in nearby communities who often phone him to voice curiosity and admiration about WECM. "The perimeter of what we're doing at God's Way far outreaches the four walls of the church," said Dr. Reese. "It's regional and more profound."

Pastors, churches, and congregants come to this work with differences in personal experience and belief, so it's to be expected that some might not adopt God's Way's WECM's mission wholesale. But according to Sonya, absolute buy-in isn't necessary when it comes to generating impact.

Just talking about mental health—and debunking misunderstandings about mental illness—validates people's experiences and opens the door for collaboration among churches, behavioral health providers and families to better address community needs. "We tell them that we don't have to take the lead." "They just have to take the information. Take the resources. Share with their community, their church, their youth. When you have that type of network, it helps develop you as a person, and as a community."

## Ed Stetzer

One in four pastors and congregants suffer from mental illness. In a LifeWay Research blog, Ed Stetzer shares that earlier in his life, he became aware of some mental health issues in his own family. He stated that when he became a Christian, the initial reaction regarding these issues was that if people would trust the Lord enough, they would be healed.

But let's use that same line of reasoning with a physical medical issue. You don't trust the Lord through a broken leg or arm alone. One way you trust the Lord is that you go to a doctor and you get a cast.

Ed said when he became a pastor, he was a bit naïve. He shared a story about his friend, Jim. He and Jim were praying together and reading the Scriptures together, yet when Jim was on his medication, he was healthy and whole. Ed said this was a turning point for him in understanding that one can struggle spiritually, but be physically sick, which was a major distinction. Those in ministry are numbered among the many who suffer from mental illness conditions.

# CHAPTER SIX

# THE MENTAL HEALTH OF THE PROPHET ELIJAH

*M*any spiritual leaders in the Bible struggled to obtain victory while serving faithfully. The prophet Elijah's story is just one case study model for ministry. Many pastors and church leaders can learn a valuable lesson on self-care and God's provision to take care of His own.

We will discover from Elijah's story that mental health was not uncommon then nor is it uncommon in our day now. We are all called to serve in the capacity of the Father's will for our lives. The Prophet Elijah was a powerful man of God, and God used him mightily, but ultimately, we find Elijah depleted, mentally, physically, and emotionally drained. I feel that way at times.

Many pastors today suffer in silence with mental health issues. It is crystal clear that the Bible speaks of servants like Elijah, the prophet of God, and King David, a man after God's own heart. And the list goes on of many others who have served the Lord. We can learn and share their transparent stories around mental health-related issues.

The Lord lifted them all up and their stories are recorded to educate us. We don't have to give up on our ministry; we just need to be ministered to for a season, like God did for Elijah. Yes, we may be depleted but never disconnected from God and His love for us.

It is necessary for twenty-first-century pastors and church leaders to consider the case study on the life and ministry of Elijah. Elijah was overwhelmed by mental health even though he lived in the days of the Old Testament.

In James 5:17, James, a New Testament writer, declares that Elijah, an Old Testament prophet, is just like us. We are no different than he was— we have all experienced similar symptoms, and we all have stress-related issues, even if it is nothing more than member depression or depression over assignments.

Elijah's story is about his mental health condition while serving God in a Spirit-filled ministry and operating under a great anointing. This is nothing new; the suffering of mental illness has always been present in some form of anxiety or depression from the beginning of time, and even now as we serve God. But God does care and provide for His own.

Now in the twenty-first century in which we live, this commonality with Elijah is devastating for us to believe when we encounter the dramatic events of his life story that took place so long ago yet is relevant today. Elijah's story is found in 1 Kings chapters 17 and 19. The same God who took care of Elijah is still the one who cares today for His pastors and leaders. He still STOPS to hear us, and He is still asking the same question today, "What can I do for you?"

In the New Testament, if we would just follow the STOPS of Jesus, we would learn how Jesus showed compassion and healed those in His presence. He loved them so. Today, like our Master, we should STOP and show a more compassionate spirit toward those suffering mental illness. God stopped to restore Elijah's health and replenish his spiritual well-being.

Elijah's story is about the God in him, which made him so powerful in his moments of weakness, and how God provided for His own. The Bible reveals the mighty acts of God in Elijah's life; it is a story about how God uses His people for His glory regardless of one's mental condition or status. With God, no one is disqualified from service. Not even the pastor He calls today will be given a different task—the requirements for ministry have not changed. Pastors and leaders are not exempt from God's calling, no matter what we are experiencing in life.

Elijah's call was not based on ability, but rather his availability. Our inability or insufficiency has never mattered to God; that should be encouraging to us. The Lord told the Apostle Paul in the New Testament that His grace is sufficient in all things. It has always been, and always will be, about God's greatness and mighty acts done through His people. God is so compassionate to those who serve Him. Jesus truly is a burden lifter, a lover of our souls, and a restorer of failing health.

James says that Elijah was just like us. He suffered from anxiety, despair, unbelief, weakness, loneliness, and lack of human ability. But by living a life of persevering faith and dependence on God's grace, mercy, power, and presence, God used him to confront the wayward sinful nations while displaying God's glory and truth.

In Elijah's day, and now in our day, God still delights to pour His glory into weak vessels of clay like us. It's not what is happening to us, but rather what God is doing through us for His glory. It's never about how much God can do for us, but always about how much God can do through us.

As loyal followers of Christ, we must be willing to live for Jesus through times of tribulation as well as times of loneliness (see Acts 14:22,

John 16:32, 1 Kings 17:2-7). As followers of Christ, there will be days when we feel depleted and depraved, have dark moments, and even feel worthless at times, when our souls are crying out for immediate help and we, too, need a compassionate, caring spirit to minister to our needs.

Preachers need to be ministered to like all other people. We have our moments of despair and weakness and often cry for help silently through prayer for the strength to overcome frustrations and anxieties. Often, it is difficult to express our emotions and disdained condition while serving at church, because no one wants to be perceived as a weak and inadequate leader; we feel we must be strong among the people of God.

Pastors and church leaders at times find themselves experiencing the same symptoms as Elijah at the brook—the place where God restores our failing health and revives us for the next level of ministry. As Elijah spent time by that drying brook, he felt depleted, lonely, and miserable, but at the same time, God was preparing him for greater works.

The Bible doesn't cover up or have a hidden agenda about those great women and men who lived during the Bible days. Like us, they experienced both physical and mental conditions while being instructed by God to serve as His servant leaders.

The Bible provides for us a clear picture of those whom the Lord called and chose to use. It gives us the whole story, both the failures and achievements of their life stories. When the Bible describes the great cloud of witnesses of the Old Testament and the New Testament, it tells the unvarnished truth of their struggles in real life ministry, their temptations, their difficulties. We too in ministry have experienced the same struggles and hardships, and we are not exempt from moments of anxiety and depression.

For our benefit, God used them and raised them up during their moments of depression and anxiety. Even today as we fall in ministry because of mental illness, member depression, or anxiety, God will still raise us up to serve Him again despite our previous conditions. God will never leave us nor forsake us. Elijah did not know God was preparing him for his next great adventure.

### Elijah, a Preacher Just Like Us

Ministry can be overwhelming at times and loneliness can set in, having a deep-rooted effect and setting off a chain of events. Elijah's mental and physical condition suggests he is in a state of desperation. He is depressed, and on the run, in what we call the fight, flight, or freeze syndrome.

The story in 1 Kings 19:1–18 ends with Ahab heading back to Jezreel to bring the sad news to Jezebel. God is still in charge and Elijah is under divine surveillance, and the presence of the Lord was present to heal and save at all cost.

Are you at a point of depravity in ministry, wanting to stop right here? Elijah is so stressed out that he has given up on the belief that he can make a difference. Why did Elijah run away? Why do we cover up what is happening to us today? God knows who we are, where we are, and what we are going through, and he will provide what we need in a timely manner. Sometimes we just need to analyze what is happening to us. Note the following:

1. Elijah was not thinking rationally or realistically.

2. Elijah separated himself from those who could strengthen him. It is interesting how human nature works. When we get discouraged, we tend to withdraw from human contact, and that is often the worst thing we can do! There are those around us who are trustworthy and will offer sustainability in our time of need. It is a good practice to share our ministry work with those we have equipped to serve in

greater capacities. Our work can overwhelm us, often leaving us drained spiritually, emotionally, and mentally.

3.    Elijah's vulnerability came on the heels of a great spiritual victory.

4.    Elijah was exhausted physically and emotionally.

5.    Elijah got lost in self-pity. The Bible says, "But he himself went a day's journey into the wilderness and came and sat down under a broom tree. And he prayed that he might die, and said, 'It is enough! Now, LORD, take my life, for I am no better than my fathers!'"

Elijah's request for God to take his life does not make much sense if you think about it. He is here in the wilderness because Jezebel had threatened his life; if he wanted to die, all he had to do was stay put and Jezebel would have been more than happy to help him out. Most of us have our "desert days" of despair. The Lord promises to never leave us nor forsake us.

Elijah is well spoken of as a man of deep devotion and obedience and admired for his strong faith. But then there comes a time in his ministry describing Elijah's breakdown, humiliation, failure, and defeat, just as we often experience today—a man just like ourselves! It is alright for us as pastors to say we are not ok. What an enlightening statement to hear from our leaders for those who may be suffering while going through a mental illness.

- There are times that we get discouraged, depressed, and despondent.
- There are times when we find ourselves in the grip of despair.

- There are times when fear tries to possess us.
- There are times when doubt tries to get the best of us.
- There are times when we experience loneliness and a feeling that nobody understands us at all.

Even we as minister the gospel of our Lord and Savior, we can experience dramatic changes and cry out for human help.

## Elijah's Collapse and Restoration

In this case study, let's take a closer look at how discouraged Elijah was and the condition that he found himself in while in full ministry (preaching from the pulpit).

- He was suddenly gripped by fear and awakened. Fear is a dreadful thing, which we have all experienced in some measure of Christian devotion.
- He went into a self-imposed isolation. He was unable to bear the presence of his servant. When we are over-strained, even the presence of friends and loved ones can irritate us.
- He was overwhelmed with depression, despondency, and despair. Elijah is now sitting under a broom tree! Have you been like that? Are you under the broom tree now? Look up Psalms 42:11 and 43:5.
- He was presumptuous and unwise in his praying. He felt as the psalmist did in Psalm 55:3–8.
- He was filled with self-pity. This is always a dangerous state to get into.
- He had an unbalanced view of things. In times of overstrain and illness, everything gets out of perspective, and little

problems become greatly exaggerated in our minds. This is called overload.

- He temporarily lost his faith in God. He still believed in Him, but he could not trust Him in this emergency, so "he went to pieces."

There is little doubt that Elijah was experiencing a nervous breakdown and was even suicidal. As pastors and leaders, we are all subject, to a greater or lesser degree, to some or all the above-mentioned emotions or reactions. So how did Elijah fall into this depression that led to his breakdown?

- He was mentally overworked. For those three and a half years, he had experienced terrific tension, culminating in the great victory on Mount Carmel and the slaughter of those false prophets.
- He was physically exhausted. Not only had the experiences of the past years made heavy demands upon his body, but now he had just taken about a twenty-mile hike toward the Mediterranean Sea.
- He was spiritually out of touch. "When he saw *that his condition was depleted* and began to cry out in his moment of despair." We see a similar comparison in Matthew 14:30. Elijah took his eyes off the Lord and looked at his circumstances and the threats of Jezebel. If you want to be depressed, fearful, filled with self-pity, etc., take your eyes off the Lord and look at your circumstances and the problems of this weary world. just take a good look at yourself!

So, the three basic reasons for Elijah's collapse are that he was sick mentally, physically, and spiritually. These must be considered together, for the mental affects the spiritual, the physical affects the mental, and so forth. This leads to burn out, blow out, and cry out.

Now let's look at what the Lord prescribed as a cure to set him back on the road to recovery. Consider that even today, God offers us the same support and help while serving in His kingdom.

Elijah was physically exhausted, so the Lord attended to the needs of his body. Look up Psalm 103:14. God prescribed food, sleep, and plenty of fresh air. He gave His servant a month and a half off as a job recovery package! It is essential to pay attention to these three simple rules for bodily health: (1) daily nourishing food; (2) regular and sufficient sleep; (3) fresh air, exercise, and relaxation.

1. Elijah was mentally overworked, so the Lord dealt with his mind. His mental outlook was distorted and unbalanced, so after a month and a half of rest and care, healthy food, and fresh air, the Lord came to him and repeated His question, "Elijah, what are you doing here?" God's objective was to cause Elijah to face realities, face his fears, and face his problems, even as we should do today.

2. Elijah was out of touch spiritually, so the Lord dealt with his soul. He gave him a wonderful vision of His power, glory, and tenderness. 1 Kings 19:11–12 run parallel to Psalm 46:10. Elijah needed physical restoration and mental renewal, but most of all, he needed a spiritual revival. Even today, ministry can be taxing and overwhelming, and it is necessary to take a few days off from time to time for spiritual restoration and renewal.

Sometimes we forget the faithfulness of our Lord. God seems remote and far removed from our struggles. We ask, "Where is God in all this?" The Lord knows when we need Him the most and will send a provision to restore our mental and emotional well-being.

Life often seems so relentless, and there is no exception for those in ministry. We can all feel somewhat hopeless at times, and there appears to be an erosion of our stamina and strength in the struggle to carry on day after day. There seems so much more pain than pleasure in our everyday lives.

Sometimes forgetting the unremitting faithfulness of God to us in the past, we focus only on the futility and frustrations of our present-day experiences. Yes, there are times when one can see no hope or cheering prospects for the future. Let us further consider how God deals with Elijah's depression and emotional well-being. Everyone needs time out every now and then.

1.  God allowed Elijah time to rest and receive refreshment.

2.  As he slept under a tree, suddenly an angel touched him and said, "Arise and eat."

3.  Then he looked, and there by his head was a cake baked on coals, and a jar of water. So, he ate and drank and lay down again.

4.  The angel of the LORD came back the second time, touched him, and said, "Arise and eat, because the journey is too great for you." Elijah's ministry was not over. God is not through with us yet.

5.  So, he arose, and ate and drank; and he was strengthened by the food that God had provided for him, sustaining him those forty days and forty nights as far as Horeb, the mountain of God.

6.    The principle here is simple—to overcome stress, we need to rest our bodies. Sometimes the most spiritual thing we can do is not take on another project but kick back and rest. Delegate some work to your helpers; Elijah failed to take his helper with him.

7.    Elijah had spent a great deal of energy fighting for God and now he is physically and emotionally spent.

God provided for his physical needs; he provided food and water and allowed Elijah to get much-needed rest. God did not even begin to deal with Elijah's depression or wrong thinking until he was rested and refreshed. He confronted Elijah with truth.

Upon arriving on the mountain, Elijah took up residence in a cave. There, God began to deal with Elijah's threefold need:

1.    He needed to face his fears. God asks, "What are you doing here, Elijah?" It was not that the Lord did not know. This question was not for God's benefit, but for Elijah's. The question is twofold: First, "Elijah, what are you doing?" Obviously, Elijah is in a self-imposed isolation, brooding and indulging in self-pity.

2.    The second time God asked the same question, "What are you doing here? Here is not the place I command for you. Here is not the place of blessing." Elijah responds by saying, "I have been very zealous for the LORD God of hosts; for the children of Israel have forsaken your covenant, torn down your altars, and killed your prophets with the sword. I alone am left; and they seek to take my life." Note that Elijah completely missed the point here.

3.   God asked a present tense question, "What are you
     doing here?" Elijah answered with a past tense response.
     Everything he spoke about was in the past. Elijah did have
     a tremendous past, but the question is, "What are you
     doing now?"

Sometimes we are so busy in the King's business that we neglect the King. There are times life gets taxing with its stress, burdens, and pressures, and we lose our focus. We desperately need to refocus on God. Psalm 46:10 says, "Be still and know that I am God." We must learn as Elijah did to look for God in the trivial things of this life.

If we pay attention, we will begin to see God in our everyday life, in a phone call of encouragement offered to someone, an unexpected kindness or a card in the mail, an answered prayer, or someone just calling or showing up at the right moment. God always speaks loudly enough for the willing ear to hear. Elijah needed a fresh revelation from God at times, and we do as well. Just listen to the voice of God and hear His instructions for you.

## Lessons from Elijah's Story

From the pulpit to the pews, many are facing mental health issues, and many more will be affected by those who respond inappropriately to those with mental illness. They've heard it all before: "Just pull yourself together and pray more faithfully," "You feel like this because your faith is weak," "I can't see anything wrong with you. Cheer up; this problem will pass," "You will be ok."

We understand that everyone's circumstances can be different, but just knowing someone cares can make a monumental difference. We need caring and not judging, not criticizing, not shaming, not pretending. Life doesn't always go the way we plan. Stress, anxiety, and depression are illnesses, not a mark of a faith lying shattered on the floor. All of us know that it probably takes greater faith to hold on to God in the depths of depression than it does when everything's hunky-dory.

Maybe that's why God honors Elijah's detour to Horeb rather than condemn him for it; the prophet runs away and wants to die in a dead zone, but God still shows up, God is still on Elijah side, and God is on our side this very day. We might feel depleted and ashamed at times but never disconnected from the love of God.

There will be people in our pews and pulpits whose secret journey into our sanctuaries and into the pastoral office has been just as fraught as Elijah's walk to the holy mountain. And that's when we must turn down the noise and let the whispers of God drown out our biases, our preconceptions, our judgments, and our inability to see the pain in front of us, and just love.

We all need to clearly understand that what is happening to others can happen to every one of us as well. It's not just those who can't face waking up in the morning who need to hear the still, small voice of God. It's not just those who are scared all the time, not just those who can't shut up the stressed-out babel in their minds—it's all of us because any one of us could soon find ourselves in the same situation. We all have our weak moments, but that doesn't mean that we are not strong or invaluable to the church.

Anyone of us could find ourselves sitting on a mountain, so let's work to make it easier for people to hear God's voice over the earthquake. It's an opportunity to survive the rushing flood waters; let's work to make sure people have the help they need to climb the mountain so they don't sit up there feeling alone and in a state of spiritual, physical, and mental depravity. Whom the Son sets free is free indeed.

Those of us who have a mental illness are sometimes told our mental illness is our fault because we lack faith. This is not the case. Mental illness is a biological disorder and can affect anyone, just as it affected Elijah in his spiritual leadership role.

When pastors, church leaders, and those serving in authority chose to be vocal and visible in sharing their stories about their own recovery and daily experiences, it is a strength and support to others who suffer from mental illnesses, and something powerful begins to happen. When pastors and leaders fight for the mental wellness of the people who follow them, there is an igniting of hope and survival. From a pastoral point of view, there is a need to take a more proactive role in mental health concerns.

We can learn many lessons from Elijah's story. As pastors and leaders, we need to take care of ourselves physically, mentally, and spiritually. When we are tired, we need to get enough rest and sleep. And we need to eat the right foods to give us energy. If we neglect personal care, neglect, anxiety, and denial will lead to blow out and burn out.

We can conclude that in Elijah's depression, he had a desire to die, which is not entirely a spiritual issue. Rather, his physical exhaustion, his cognitive beliefs, and his social isolation influenced his emotions and his spirit. Because he was tired, misinformed, and alone, he was mentally and spiritually unhealthy.

So, what can we learn from Elijah story about emotional wellness and having a good mental health plan for ourselves and our congregants? The next time you're feeling stressed, anxious, or discouraged, ask yourself if you're exhausted, believing a lie, or isolated. If so, find some extra time to rest, eat some healthy food, go fishing, think about the truth, and connect with a friend. Leave your cell phone behind; God is speaking and restoring you. If those activities don't help, then call your doctor, your pastor, a counselor, or a friend. Live a better day. We only get one life, one mind, and one body. "He refreshes my soul and restores my failing health" (Psalm 23:3).

# CHAPTER SEVEN

# MEDITATIONS AND MEDICATIONS

*O*ver the years, there has been much study and argument over theological concepts and psychological studies. The Bible clearly states that all things work together. I believe God intended for meditations and medications to complement each other for the greater purpose, for the total healing of mind, body, and soul. God's purpose for humanity was to meet the whole need of mankind. The Lord has always been concerned about the person, that one be in good health even as their soul prospers.

Medicine is a gift from God to help the process of healing. Humankind is both flesh and spirit by the divine nature of God. Because of who God created us to be, we need spiritual, physical, and mental healing. Therefore, our approach to healing must be multifaced, using a diversity of resources and medical helps.

Nowhere in Scripture does God command Christians to avoid doctors or medicine. In fact, medical wisdom is often acknowledged as a gift from

God for the benefit of people. The Bible is loaded with examples of various practices and Scriptures.

Let's begin in Genesis 17:10-14, where the Lord commands circumcision to Abraham. God ordained this minor surgery for a specific, spiritual purpose; nevertheless, this example demonstrates that relying on a medical procedure isn't contrary to obeying God. In fact, it's necessary to do both, always obey God and follow the doctor's instructions for healing.

In Genesis 50:2, there are physicians called Joseph's "servants," and the word for physicians is the same word used to described God as our "healer" in Exodus 15:26. Once again, the implication is that physicians are doing an excellent work for God's people as an extension of God's own healing ministry.

Proverbs 17:22 states, "A merry heart does good like a medicine." This verse presents medicine in a positive light as a metaphor for a happy heart. If our reliance on medicine was contrary to faith, then the Word of God would never have used it as a metaphor for a glad heart.

In Isaiah 38:21, we find the prophet prescribing a cataplasm as a medicinal remedy for Hezekiah's boil. While God directs all healing, the cataplasm clearly demonstrates that God uses medical procedures at times to deliver the healing He provides. This is convincing evidence that we may be healed by God through sound medical practices!

In other examples, we find in Jeremiah 8:22 a statement that Gilead approves of physicians, albeit metaphorically. Then Jeremiah 30:13 equates the lack of medicine with a lack of healing, and Jeremiah 51:8 says medicine is the way for Babylon to be healed. Although these examples are spiritual metaphors, they only work as metaphors *because* they rest upon the fact of God's gracious provision of medical treatments available for our benefit.

One final verse from the Old Testament is especially telling. Ezekiel 47:12 says healing medicine will be made from the leaves of trees that are nourished by waters from the new temple in the New Jerusalem. Revelation 22:2 also describes the tree of healing in the New Jerusalem, suggesting that medicinal tools are an important part of God's purpose.

We are not suggesting that healing is accomplished through medicine alone (nor that our resurrected bodies will suffer from physical ailments), but rather that God supports the life of our bodies in a variety of physical ways, including through food, water, rest and, at times, medicine. If you are interested in learning more about why a healing tree exists in the New Jerusalem, God has a plan for the total healing of mind, body, and soul. We shall be bathed in the ease of heavenly rest.

Looking to the New Testament there is a scripture where Jesus Christ said in Luke 4:23, "Physician heal yourself" and applied it to Himself. Another scripture found in Luke 5:31 says that they who are whole need not a physician. In no case do we find Christ disapproving of medicines or physicians. In fact, Colossians 4:14 shares that one of the Gospel writers, Luke, was a "beloved physician" himself.

Certainly, every Christian should understand that all healing comes from God, so we can seek medical treatment knowing that the Lord often uses medicine and meditations to accomplish His healing. The book of Psalms is loaded with inspirations and blessing for the soul, which calms our fears and troubling minds.

Scripture is a powerful tool loaded with information for human cures. They are given by God to help in the healing process; however, Christians should consider the numerous aspects of healing. It doesn't mean we should stop praying, nor does it mean that our faith in God is not working. The truth is it is working for our good when we believe God and obey Him in all things. Proverbs 4:7 states, "Wisdom is the principal thing; therefore, get wisdom, and with all thy getting, get understanding."

The principle here is to understand that there is a shared responsibility of care providers for the sole purpose of total healing and health redemption, and a divine spiritual purpose for healing from a biblical perspective as well. Through it all, God is the ultimate healer in every situation. All things work together for the good of God's people.

Proverbs 4:20-23 states, "My son attend to my words, incline thine ear unto my sayings, let them not depart from thine eyes, keep them in the midst of thine heart, for they are life unto those who find them, and health to all their flesh. Keep thy heart with all diligence, for out of it are the issues of life. The word of God is a refreshing and healing spirit."

Jesus used both spiritual meditations and physical materials as medication in His healing process. "When He had spoken (meditation), He spat on the ground, and made clay of the spittle, and anointed the eyes of the blind man with clay (medication) (John 9:6).

Jesus was certainly aware of the diverse culture of His day. From His teachings, we learn the valuable spiritual lesson that sometimes we must use the resources around us to aid the healing process. The Lord Himself reserves the right to heal whomever He desires and at His appointed time. Most of the stuff that God has provided for our healing is at our disposal. Often, we hear of a discovery and breakthrough that offers some form of cure for humanity's ailments.

Here are a few additives to help us think again about mental health issues that can be addressed by both meditations and medications complementing each other in real life:

### Proverbs 17:22 KJV
A merry heart doeth good like a medicine: but a broken
spirit drieth the bones.

### Psalm 103:2–3 KJV

Bless the Lord, O my soul, and forget not all his benefits: Who forgiveth all thine iniquities; who healeth all thy diseases;

### Jeremiah 8:22 KJV

Is there no balm in Gilead; is there no physician there? why then is not the health of the daughter of my people recovered?

### 1 Timothy 5:23 KJV

Drink no longer water but use a little wine for thy stomach's sake and thine often infirmities.

### Revelation 22:2 KJV

In the midst of the street of it, and on either side of the river, was there the tree of life, which bare twelve manners of fruits, and yielded her fruit every month: and the leaves of the tree were for the healing of the nations.

### Ezekiel 47:12 KJV

And on the banks, on both sides of the river, there will grow all kinds of trees for food. Their leaves will not wither, nor their fruit fail, but they will bear fresh fruit every month, because the water for them flows from the sanctuary. Their fruit will be for food, and their leaves for healing."

### Isaiah 38:21 KJV

Now Isaiah had said, "Let them take a cake of figs and apply it to the boil, that he may recover."

### Matthew 9:12 KJV

But when he heard it, he said, "Those who are well have no need of a physician, but those who are sick.

### Luke 10:34 KJV

He went to him and bound up his wounds, pouring on oil and wine. Then he set him on his own animal and brought him to an inn and took care of him.

### Psalm 103:3 KJV

Who forgives all your iniquity, who heals all thy diseases,

### Isaiah 1:6 ESV

From the sole of the foot even to the head, there is no soundness in it, but bruises and sores and raw wounds; they are not pressed out or bound up or softened with oil.

### Psalm 147:3 ESV

He heals the brokenhearted and binds up their wounds.

### Mark 5:24–29 ESV

And he went with him. And a great crowd followed him and thronged about him. And there was a woman who had had a discharge of blood for twelve years, and who had suffered much under many physicians, and had spent all that she had, and was no better but rather grew worse. She had heard the reports about Jesus and came up behind him in the crowd and touched his garment. For she said, "If I touch even his garments, I will be made well." ...

### Psalm 30:2 ESV

O Lord my God, I cried to you for help, and you have healed me.

### 2 Chronicles 16:12 ESV

In the thirty-ninth year of his reign Asa was diseased in his feet, and his disease became severe. Yet even in his disease he did not seek the LORD but sought help from physicians.

### James 5:14 ESV

Is anyone among you sick? Let him call for the elders of the church, and let them pray over him, anointing him with oil in the name of the Lord.

### James 1:5 ESV

If any of you lacks wisdom, let him ask God, who gives generously to all without reproach, and it will be given him.

### Psalm 107:19–20 ESV

Then they cried to the Lord in their trouble, and he delivered them from their distress. He sent out his word and healed them and delivered them from their destruction.

### John 3:16 ESV

For God so loved the world, that he gave his only Son, that whoever believes in him should not perish but have eternal life.

### Luke 8:48 ESV

And he said to her, "Daughter, your faith has made you well; go in peace."

### Matthew 8:1–34 ESV

When he came down from the mountain, great crowds followed him. And behold, a leper came to him and knelt before him, saying, "Lord, if you will, you can make me clean." And Jesus stretched out his hand and touched him, saying, "I will; be clean." And immediately his leprosy was cleansed. And Jesus said to him, "See that you say nothing to anyone, but go, show yourself to the priest and offer the gift that Moses commanded, for a proof to them." When he entered Capernaum, a centurion came forward to him, appealing to him, ...

### Luke 4:23 ESV

And he said to them, "Doubtless you will quote to me this proverb, 'Physician, heal yourself.' What we have heard you did at Capernaum, do here in your hometown as well."

### Proverbs 15:13 ESV

A glad heart makes a cheerful face, but by sorrow of heart the spirit is crushed.

### Psalm 41:3 ESV

The LORD sustains him on his sickbed; in his illness you restore him to full health.

### Mark 5:34 ESV

And he said to her, "Daughter, your faith has made you well; go in peace and be healed of your disease."

### Revelation 3:18 ESV

I counsel you to buy from me gold refined by fire, so that you may be rich, and white garments so that you may clothe yourself and the shame of your nakedness may not be seen, and salve to anoint your eyes, so that you may see.

### 3 John 1:2 ESV

Beloved, I pray that all may go well with you and that you may be in good health, as it goes well with your soul.

### 1 Corinthians 6:19–20 ESV

Or do you not know that your body is a temple of the Holy Spirit within you, whom you have from God? You are not your own, for you were bought with a price. So glorify God in your body.

### Luke 5:31 ESV

And Jesus answered them, "Those who are well have no need of a physician, but those who are sick.

### Proverbs 14:13 ESV

Even in laughter the heart may ache, and the end of joy may be grief.

### Mark 2:17 ESV

And when Jesus heard it, he said to them, "Those who are well have no need of a physician, but those who are sick. I came not to call the righteous, but sinners."

### Proverbs 4:22 ESV

For they are life to those who find them, and healing to all their flesh.

### Psalm 103:2–3 ESV

Bless the Lord, O my soul, and forget not all his benefits, who forgives all your iniquity, who heals all your diseases,

and behold, it was very good. And there was evening and there was morning, the sixth day.

### John 5:1–47 ESV

After this there was a feast of the Jews, and Jesus went up to Jerusalem. Now there is in Jerusalem by the Sheep Gate a pool, in Aramaic called Bethesda, which has five roofed colonnades. In these lay a multitude of invalids—blind, lame, and paralyzed. One man was there who had been an invalid for thirty-eight years. When Jesus saw him lying there and knew that he had already been there a long time, he said to him, "Do you want to be healed?" ...

### Mark 5:26 ESV

And who had suffered much under many physicians, and had spent all that she had, and was no better but rather grew worse.

### James 5:13 ESV

Is anyone among you suffering? Let him pray. Is anyone cheerful? Let him sing praise.

### 2 Corinthians 13:9 ESV

For we are glad when we are weak, and you are strong. Your restoration is what we pray for.

### John 3:16–17 ESV

"For God so loved the world, that he gave his only Son, that whoever believes in him should not perish but have eternal life. For God did not send his Son into the world to condemn the world, but in order that the world might be saved through him.

### Matthew 8:16–17 ESV

That evening they brought to him many who were oppressed by demons, and he cast out the spirits with a word and healed all who were sick. This was to fulfill what was spoken by the prophet Isaiah: "He took our illnesses and bore our diseases."

### Mark 16:15–18 ESV

And he said to them, "Go into all the world and proclaim the gospel to the whole creation. Whoever believes and is baptized will be saved, but whoever does not believe will be condemned. And these signs will accompany those who believe: in my name they will cast out demons; they will speak in new tongues; they will pick up serpents with their hands; and if they drink any deadly poison, it will not hurt them; they will lay their hands on the sick, and they will recover."

Religion and medicine are bound to intersect at some point. It is important that a patient's spiritual values are respected and considered when transitioning to professional referrals. It's a matter of teamwork and support. Some religious values may conflict with medical decisions, but there is no need to fear. God is in control and works through all human interventions for the good of His people. I believe that, ultimately, be it spiritual or professional helps, all anyone expects is that we behave with integrity.

Ed Stetzer wrote an article on mental illness and medication as opposed to spiritual struggles and biblical counseling. Here is what he said. "Among evangelicals, you will find some who are open to dealing with mental illness as a physiological reality, but you will also find others who think they can gain no value from listening to the world."

One might wonder why we can't just read enough Scripture or pray enough. Why can't that cure us? Because in some cases, there are physical, chemical, or physiological issues. Yes, prayer can help, and yes, God does still heal in miraculous ways.

But often, more prayer and more faith are not the only remedies for mental illness. Medicine is still needed at times for spiritual, mental, and physical healing. God created balms, gums, oils, herbs, foods, wine, and all sorts of medications for healing. The Scriptures declare that all He made was good. Sometimes we must decide between walking on feet or riding in a car—it's about a choice of what's most helpful. Some would just rather swim than get on the boat crossing to the other side, but that's just human nature. People, in general, have unique perspectives.

Most people would agree that, in many ways, we are an overmedicated society. We must be careful in how we prescribe and administer medications, but this does not mean we should be afraid of medical interventions entirely.

Mental health is a spiritual issue in some instances, but it can also be a medical issue. We should recognize and admit that the faith community is sometimes unsure of how to deal with this tension. All truth is God's truth, and both spiritual truths and medical truths are part of dealing with these issues.

David Murray explains another helpful distinction. He says if there's one thing we can all do, it's to avoid making our own experience the rule for others. That's the most common mistake he has seen people make. He agrees that he himself fell into the same situation. Just because medication worked for you does not mean it will work for everyone else. Just because biblical counseling alone worked for you doesn't mean it's the complete answer for everyone else. God is for all of us, and He desires that all prosper and be in good health even as our soul prospers.

Just because you've never been depressed doesn't mean depression does not exist. Cases are so different, and causes are so complex, that we need to exercise charity, sympathy, and patience in all our dealings with one another. Everyone is unique.

David mentioned that he could only see mental illness and the benefits of medication through others in his family and church. Part of the reason it's difficult to acknowledge these facts is that there can be a perception that Christians shouldn't have these issues.

Part of our belief system is that God changes everything. Sometimes we ask, "Why hasn't God fixed this?" But that stigma can be a hindrance instead of a help.

Some will respond to our questioning by saying it is all because of sin, a lack of faith, or a lack of repentance. Jesus said in John 9:3, "It was not that this man sinned, or his parents, but that the work of God might be displayed in him."

Yes, there are consequences for sin. Jesus Himself is the balm (medicine) of Gilead that heals the sin-sick soul. But someone's struggle with anxiety, depression or another form of mental illness does not mean it is the result of something they've done or not done. There is a difference between sin sickness and mental illness. The end result is that all need healing of the soul.

Tim Keller has written a helpful article on the four models of counseling in pastoral ministries. He mentioned that we must beware of giving people the impression that through individual repentance of sin, they should be able to undo their personal problems. Obviously, we should not go to the other unbiblical extreme of refusing to acknowledge personal responsibility for sinful behavior.

While we can't fall into the reductionism of believing all problems are chemically based and require medication, we also cannot fall into the reductionism of believing all problems are simply a matter of lacking spiritual disciplines, or sinful activity. Every case is what it is, and we should not read anything else into it.

Schizophrenia, bipolar depression, and a host of other psychological problems are rooted in physiological problems that call for medical treatment, not simple talk therapy.

Keller is on point that both ends of the spectrum are dangerous places to counsel from. It's not always a result of sin, yet the answer is not always medication. Healing is always God's desire and purpose for us.

We sometimes think that because Christ lives in us, everything in us, things in our hearts and our minds, should be fixed and made perfect in this lifetime. As a Christian, I know that Christ does change all things. In Him we live, move, and have our being. Life is a work in progress and often must go through its process to achieve perfection. Know that eternal life is the ultimate goal that God has predetermined as eternal wellness.

But to use the illustration that life is a process, if a leg or arm is broken, we still need a cast for about six to eight weeks to heal. The idea of pulling yourself up by your bootstraps because you broke your leg or arm doesn't always work. You're still going to fall, and your leg will not heal correctly on its own. Now if you were experiencing a chemical imbalance, you might still need external help. We need to extend the belief that physical illness and mental illness can and should be treated—there is just a difference in the care needed.

There are spiritual struggles. People do go through spiritual darkness, and all people of faith should recognize that. It's not perfectly delineated, but there is a difference between a spiritual struggle and a physical mental sickness. They do relate, yet they are not the same.

With spiritual struggles or personal struggles, what some would call downtime or a meltdown, there is a need for faith-based counseling, which is a wonderful tool. But, at the same time, personal and spiritual struggles are not the same thing as mental illness. And it's exceedingly important for us to identify the difference between them.

If I'm struggling with grief, with sin, or with any host of issues, having people who can encourage me or even counselors in the Christian tradition are wonderful. But there is a difference between that and mental illness, which is a physiological reality.

We wouldn't shame someone for getting a virus or a runny nose. Why do we shame someone for having a chemical imbalance that leads him or her into a lifelong struggle with depression? Often there is an expectation because we really do believe, as the Apostle Paul writes to the Philippians, that "I can do all things through Christ who strengthens me."

But that doesn't mean we don't need the support of the church and community. It doesn't mean we don't need medical help. But we can do all things through Christ who strengthens us.

I may sound like a broken record, but it bears repeating. People are crying out for help, and we cannot afford to be ignorant or afraid to reach out in total support. Christians must break the stigma and shame of mental illness.

Steve Austin is a family man, writer, speaker, and advocate of second chances. A native of Birmingham, Alabama, Steve blogs regularly. Here is what he says about his daily mental health journey.

Anxiety has been my constant companion for as long as I can remember. For several years, I lived under a cloud of shame because of it. I believed I would never find true belonging if anyone knew the factual issues I faced daily.

Until I could no longer hide. A failed suicide attempt forced me to face myself. At first, all I wanted to do was disconnect from anyone and anything that seemed more "normal" than me. And everyone seems more normal than you feel when you've just been discharged from the psych ward. I didn't want anyone to know my story or the details of the journey that eventually landed me in an ICU. I didn't want my family to know, and I certainly didn't want to face the church.

Like so many others, I thought life came with two choices: be a normal Christian guy or be crazy. I felt stuck. Lost.

I wonder if the Prodigal Son was feeling like me. The parable certainly implies he was humiliated. If the Prodigal Son had been able to work through the smothering lies that come with shame, would he have come home sooner? I've heard others ask it this way: "If the Prodigal Son had Xanax, would he have ever come home?"

Early in recovery, my biggest struggle with returning to the church was getting past that sense of not being good enough.

My fear of being compared to all the other "normal" Christians made it very hard to believe in a Father who was inherently good, patient, and kind.

The Church had been my home for nearly three decades, but after such a massive personal failure, I wasn't sure how I fit into it anymore. From my own experience, the church knows how to deal with addiction, adultery, and anger. But mental illness dumbfounds them.

I am from a spirit-filled church, where we believe in anointing oils and prayers of faith. In this world, medication for emotional issues is not really accepted. I can talk about addiction, but if I mention medication for mental illness, a team of people preps to cast out a demon.

Nearly four years into recovery, I often wonder if we would have the same response to a Christian with cancer? Sweet older women think they're being encouraging when they tell you the freedom that Jesus can bring, so you'll no longer be dependent on medication. But their message just causes our shame to simmer even more.

With both mental illness and cancer, you can't see the disease. But, while it is perfectly OK for a cancer patient to have chemo, it is not always acceptable for someone with a mental illness to take a prescription to address the chemical imbalance that dramatically affects their life. I long for the day when I can comfortably say, "My hope is built on nothing less than Jesus' blood and good prescription drugs."

As it stands, the church's response ostracizes people who need faith and community the most. Even well-meaning pastors, offering a prayer of faith at an altar call, will say God can "heal the minds" of those with anxiety and depression. Even if God can, this kind of talk just makes us want to slink back into the shadows and disappear. Healing sounds so great, but comfort and inclusion sound even better. The Church's attempts to encourage or heal causes even more shame for a person who already feels they are not enough.

I want the church to do more. That might include some research, some reaching out. What would happen if the church said to those with mental illness, "You are different, but not less"? What if the church could break down walls of shame and begin a healthy dialogue? Isn't that what every person wants—to be heard and respected? To feel as though we belong?

In my experience, mental illness causes a person to look at a certain point in time thru a zoom lens. As emotions go up, rational thinking goes down. As the church, this is the perfect opportunity to offer some of that "peace that passes understanding" to someone who feels the constriction of anxiety around their throat. Helping someone who is panicked to slow down, look at the larger picture, find God in the ordinary moments, and see all they do have to be thankful for just might save a life.

If the Prodigal Son had had Xanax, would he have come back home? Maybe so, maybe not. Or maybe he would have never left at all. Maybe he would have been able to steady his mind long enough to recognize how good his life already was. Maybe he would have thrown his arms around his dad and joined him in work rather than floundering and acting so impulsively.

It is impossible to think about a hopeful future and a caring support system when we feel ostracized and defensive. The Father is standing, arms wide open, waiting to embrace all His children who are burdened, weary, and anxious. It's time for the church to stop acting like the older brother, and instead, embrace those who have wandered home after a long journey. The Father's love has everything to do with inclusion.

The Scripture says, "Finally, brethren, whatsoever things are true, whatsoever things are honest, whatsoever things are just, whatsoever things are pure, whatsoever thing are lovely, whatsoever things are of good report, if there be any virtue, if there be any praise, think on these things" (Philippians 4:8).

# CHAPTER EIGHT

# MENTAL HEALTH INCLUSION WITHIN OUR WALLS AND BEYOND

*W*ell Inclusion is the story of how outsiders can become insiders. Everyone is seeking relationships, and no one wants a distant relationship. As Christians, we are called to use the power of relationships. No matter who or what we are, everyone wants to be loved unconditionally and with integrity. Inclusion is the spiritual right of every believer as well as a universal right. Everyone has access and equal opportunity to what is best for them, and the right to be treated irrespective of race, gender, disability, or medical or religious status.

Diversity means we are different, but it doesn't mean we do not belong together or share like concerns and needs. We all cry and hurt the same, and we all are a part of God's plan. Spiritually speaking, God's plan for inclusion was to get everyone walking in the same direction, having all things in common, fellowshipping and breaking bread together, and having favor with all people (Acts 2).

There is a growing need within the local church, the need of accessibility for all congregants to participate in worship activities, volunteer in ministry helps, provide the opportunity to share their stories, and be recognized as a gifted part in the body of Christ, given freely in service for God's glory. This is all part of the Christian redemption story.

Our words and actions limit the movement of total inclusion in the lives of others at church and beyond. We must never allow our conscious or unconscious circles of exclusion to prevent us from reaching out to people. The stigma around mental health can be removed through talk therapy, destroying doubt, and giving hope to everyone that have experienced some form of discrimination. We need to understand that this is a people journey, and not one should be left alone because they are different in culture. This is our journey, and we are stronger together.

Too many churches and community services have failed to empower those suffering and struggling with mental health problems to get their life back on track and get back into the church and community as active participants. Every day, we should tell someone we love them. Love has a way of conquering in all things.

One major shift in health and wellness is the inclusion of mental health care for everyone. Wellness is no longer simply just exercise and nutrition, but also positive reinforcement for loved ones, being mindful of the needs of people in general, freedom and relaxation for all, and self-care. Pastors are included as people that need care as well.

There is a strong link between the recovery process and social inclusion. A key role for services is to support people in regaining their place in the church and communities where they live and participating in mainstream activities and opportunities along with everyone else. A growing body of evidence demonstrates that participating in kingdom work, social work, educational, training, volunteering, and employment opportunities can support the process of individual recovery.

It is vital that we change how we look at mental health because it will impact how church life should look and how communities can change how they develop programs and job-related issues as a part of the inclusion initiative. We were all created to worship, to work, to love, and to care one for another.

Sometimes we allow pride and prejudice to destroy our sense of unity among people in general. There are countless examples throughout the Bible where God uses kindness, forgiveness, friendships, and relationships to reach out to hurting humanity. Let's consider these Scriptures as examples of Christian inclusion:

### Romans 12:15–16 KJV

We are to rejoice with those who rejoice, weep with those who weep. Live in harmony with one another. Do not be haughty but associate with the lowly. Never be wise in your own sight. Repay no one evil for evil but give thought to do what is honorable in the sight of all. If possible, so far as it depends on you, live peaceably with all.

### Galatians 3:28 KJV

There is neither Jew nor Greek, there is neither bond nor free, there is neither male nor female: for ye are all one in Christ Jesus.

### 1 Corinthians 12:12–27 KJV

For just as the body is one and has many members, and all the members of the body, though many, are one body, so it is with Christ.13 For in one Spirit we were all baptized into one body—Jews or Greeks, slaves or free—and all were made to drink of one Spirit. For the body does not consist of one member but of any. If the foot should say, "Because I am not a hand, I do not belong to the body," that would not make it any less a part of the body. And if the ear should say, "Because I am not an eye, I do not belong to the body," that would not make it any less a part of the body. If the whole body were an eye, where would be the sense of hearing? If the whole body were an ear, where would be the sense of smell? But as it is, God arranged the members in the body, each one of them, as he chose. 19 If all were a single member, where would the body be? As it is, there are many parts, yet one body. The eye cannot say to the hand, "I have no need of you," nor again the head to the feet, "I have no need of you." On the contrary, the parts of the body that seem to be weaker are indispensable, and on those parts of the body that we think less honorable we bestow the greater honor, and our unpresentable parts are treated with greater modesty, which our more presentable parts do not require. But God has so composed the body, giving greater honor to the part that lacked it, that there may be no division in the body, but that the members may have the same care for one another. If one member suffers, all suffer together; if one member is honored, all rejoice together. Now you are the body of Christ and individually members of it.

### Romans 3:23 KJV

For all have sinned and fall short of the glory of God,

### John 3:16 KJV

For God so loved the world, that he gave his only Son, that whoever believes in him should not perish but have eternal life.

*Ephesians 4:25 KJV*

Therefore, having put away falsehood, let each one of you speak the truth with his neighbor, for we are members one of another.

*Matthew 25:31–46 KJV*

When the Son of Man comes in his glory, and all the angels with him, then he will sit on his glorious throne. Before him will be gathered all the nations, and he will separate people one from another as a shepherd separates the sheep from the goats. And he will place the sheep on his right, but the goats on the left. Then the King will say to those on his right, "Come, you who are blessed by my Father, inherit the kingdom prepared for you from the foundation of the world. For I was hungry, and you gave me food, I was thirsty, and you gave me drink, I was a stranger and you welcomed me." "When did we do these things?" Jesus said, "When you did it unto the least, you did it unto me."

*Acts 10:47 ESV*

Can anyone withhold water for baptizing these people, who have received the Holy Spirit just as we have?

*Hebrews 13:2 ESV*

Do not neglect to show hospitality to strangers, for thereby some have entertained angels unawares.

*John 5:24 ESV*

Truly, truly, I say to you, whoever hears my word and believes him who sent me has eternal life. He does not come into judgment but has passed from death to life.

### Colossians 1:16–17 ESV

For by him all things were created, in heaven and on earth, visible and invisible, whether thrones or dominions or rulers or authorities all things were created through him and for him. And he is before all things, and in him all things hold together.

### Ephesians 4:32 ESV

Be kind to one another, tenderhearted, forgiving one another, as God in Christ forgave you.

### Romans 15:7 ESV

Therefore welcome one another as Christ has welcomed you, for the glory of God.

# CHAPTER NINE

# MENTAL HEALTH PLAN / THE HEALTHY CHURCH MODEL

*I* begin this chapter with an evaluation question that poses a challenge to every congregant. Is regular church life healthy for people with mental illness? This evaluation question is drawn from the very word of God. I believe every church should take into consideration the words of the Apostle Paul as he instructs the church to do for others. Romans 12:9-21 and Titus 2:7 shine the light on what is required of all believers, especially around church life, among the household of faith, as a sure indicator of genuine integrity.

Romans 12:9-21 lists the marks of the true Christian. We are being highlighted that men may see our good works and glorify our Father, which is in heaven:

[9] Let love be genuine. Abhor what is evil; hold fast to what is good.
[10] Love one another with brotherly affection. Outdo one another in showing honor.

[11] Do not be slothful in zeal, be fervent in spirit, serve the Lord.

[12] Rejoice in hope, be patient in tribulation, be constant in prayer.

[13] Contribute to the needs of the saints and seek to show hospitality.

[14] Bless those who persecute you; bless and do not curse them.

[15] Rejoice with those who rejoice, weep with those who weep.

[16] Live in harmony with one another. Do not be haughty but associate with the lowly. Never be wise in your own sight.

[17] Repay no one evil for evil but give thought to do what is honorable in the sight of all.

[18] If possible, so far as it depends on you, live peaceably with all.

[19] Beloved, never avenge yourselves, but leave it to the wrath of God, for it is written," Vengeance is mine, I will repay, says the Lord."

[20] To the contrary, "if your enemy is hungry, feed him; if he is thirsty, give him something to drink; for by so doing you will heap burning coals on his head."

[21] Do not be overcome by evil but overcome evil with good. (ESV)

Titus 2:7-8 states, "Show yourself in all respects to be a model of good works, and in your teaching show integrity, dignity, and sound speech that cannot be condemned, so that an opponent may be put to shame, having nothing evil to say about us" (ESV).

These Scriptures serve as a creative purpose-driven activity among congregants that leads to a healthy and stigma-free gathering of the saints and will be recognized within the communities where we live. Every church needs a mental health plan that is emotionally healthy for the entire church practice in all aspects of its ministries. We may not have it all together, but together we have it all. We are stronger together. We will never know who in the room can help us until we talk.

Church life is not always a welcome package to all believers. Over the last several years, I have asked members of various churches to explain how they are accepted or rejected, what does treatment at church look like, and what help is available to them while experiencing mental health in their local churches?

Most say they have shared their struggles with their pastor, small group leaders, or a friend at church. Some wish they hadn't shared their story of mental illness with anyone. They felt alienated, spiritually defective, and rejected, often feeling alone while at church. They say there is just too much disparity around the church when it comes to mental health and how we are made to feel.

Many feel ignored and long for true friendship at church and in the community. They don't feel the need to be preached at, just to be loved and accepted in the beloved community of the church at heart. Some said they don't need a sermon. They are saved but not safe. We are preaching love but not living in love.

They just need all believers to see them as people who love and trust God as their Savior too. They want to be treated as people who need a hug or a word of encouragement and to build lasting relationships that are meaningful and purposeful.

Because of the stigma within our four walls at church, many people of faith are too ashamed, guilty, or embarrassed to risk revealing their struggles with mental illness. Thank God that there are churches that are both emotionally and mentally healthy for those who struggle with mental illness. However, there remains a work in progress around mental health issues and ever learning trends, development, and personalization in knowing that one size doesn't always fit all. The church should be open for business every day.

The church is still the first place where people can experience emotional healing and support. We know from whom our help comes. "In Him we live, move, and have our being" according to Acts 17:28 KJV.

The healthy church knows what to look for and the values of member inclusion at its best and can see the bigger picture of what church life really looks like. The Good Samaritan provides a model for how churches can minister to those with mental illness.

The Good Samaritan did not jump to any conclusions. He saw the injured man where he was and ministered to him where he was. Perhaps the Good Samaritan could "see" him because the Good Samaritan had been through some things himself. Perhaps he, too, had been victimized and left on the side of a lonely, dusty road. Perhaps someone in his family had been helped by someone that refused to pass by on the other side.

Many people in churches have been through issues themselves or in their families. If these experiences were handled in a healthy way, they can prepare someone to minister to another in need, without discrimination or being judgmental about things we believe to be non-cost effective. Coming from a place of pain or dysfunction may sharpen your vision for those on the side of the road. It doesn't matter who you are—if you allow God to help you through your pain, God will always send someone to your side of the road.

Helpful churches try to receive at least minimal knowledge about mental illness and symptoms. Numerous health issues, side effects, and even behavior problems may occur during regular church service. The helpful churches know that the "bad child" may have attention deficit disorder, which can masquerade as behavior problems due to impulsive behavior, hyperactivity, and an inability to focus on non-interesting topics.

These kids know right from wrong and often acknowledge their mistakes. Yet they can't seem to help themselves at times. There appears to be a medical problem with how the dopamine systems react to their frontal lobes. Pastors and church leaders need continuous training, and to further educate themselves about mental health signs, symptoms, and human behavior at church, to minister in a more holistic manner.

The Good Samaritan was a safe person who did not rob the man of whatever dignity he had left on his side of the road. He assessed the man's situation and gave him what he could at the time. He was not traumatized into inaction by his fear of the unknown. He partnered with someone, the innkeeper, who could provide what he was not trained to provide. Most times, the innkeepers are our professional helps that can provide the necessary support to wholeness.

Mental health professionals serve in the innkeeper role for many churches and communities alike. The innkeeper does their job in partnership with the Good Samaritan, who never abandons the injured man but walks beside him for total support. The Good Samaritan takes ownership of the situation and comes back to check on the wounded man. It is a blessing when the church honors Hebrews 13:5, where it says, "I will never leave them or forsake them."

Innkeepers are varied. Sometimes they are psychiatrists, prescribing medications for mood and anxiety problems; others are specialists with specific treatment plans.

Some innkeepers are devout believers and Christian health care providers that offer outstanding service. Yet there is a need for dialogue that supports a unified effort around mental health as a team mission initiative. The local church can also be classified as the innkeeper position in Christ, where the body of Christ is complete in its mission and purpose of how we compassionately serve our congregants and continue to support them through other professional helps as the need arises.

Healthy churches should be classified as a safe place for mental health. Every church needs to have a mental health plan that is common to every need that presents itself as a way of life in the body of Christ.

The church that effectively ministers to those in emotional distress has a plan. The church must understand that these are our people and our families. Scripture says we are members in particular. They are not *those* people who are sitting over there. A part of the church plan is to begin developing relationships with our local mental health, faith-based communities before we need them.

A wrap-around plan must be implemented, where people can help develop those training sessions, create helpful interventions, and determine how they can be implemented and evaluated as helpful to our congregants and community.

The church must identify the mental health resources in our communities and beyond and begin to meet with them and have a meaningful dialogue about mental health issues. The local church is responsible for encouraging a healthy dialogue to ascertain how the mental health professional would approach a person of faith.

The Good Samaritan is a good model for an effective mental health plan. The church can and should continue to shepherd the spiritual status of the person through this process, with assistance from a Christian counselor, as needed. Effective churches encourage their members to get complete assessments and do not make assumptions.

They serve their congregants, even if that means taking someone to the barber shop, hairdresser, a dining date, cutting someone's grass, or just speaking or representing someone in need of our immediate assistance. What we do for others often makes a difference in their lives, especially those of the household of faith. All Christians and believers should be treated as people of God, not diagnoses. We must not neglect their spiritual or mental needs during church life activities.

The church, the very place that should offer healing, a safe place, and hope, is often the least equipped place to help. Further, it is the place least likely to be actively attended by people suffering from such conditions. That poses a problem indeed and requires a little work here at the place we call our worship center, the church at large.

In developing a mental health plan at your local church, you will need a team of devout believers who are nonjudgmental, understand the heart of the church at large, and can offer sacrificial love to everyone. At the same time, they must have the ability to explain the holistic views of the church that are related to mental health. Congregants can be over demanding and disrespectful. Those who are suffering from mental illness can be overwhelmed at times, feeling stigmatized and frightened by the words they hear and the things they see others doing, which causes separation and division at church. This can be a heartbreaking situation for so many.

It is probably an innovative idea to start with a welcome environment of acceptance, where compassionate relationships can give birth to new life. We must arrive at a place where everyone is spiritually healthy in the sense that we do no danger or harm to anyone in the church life around mental health concerns.

Every church should promote and provide opportunities with purpose for those who may be suffering from mental health problems. We must create space that promotes the purpose of ministry. Those within our church walls who are experiencing some form of mental illness should be given the opportunity to function in team ministries and be recognized as valued players and active church members.

It is the church's responsibility to include those who may be affected by mental illness, to establish a culture of spiritual enrichment that allows for regular conversations on mental health topics, coupled with other health issues such as diabetes, heart conditions, asthma, stress, anxiety, and grief from the loss of a loved one.

There should be a health care program at church. We train or instruct others to help themselves through the benevolent program. Not everyone wants a handout—they just need to be directed to the proper resources or offered employment. They just want the opportunity to work or serve like everyone else. Here at God's Way, we have members in the choir who can't talk but are in harmony. Yes, they can't talk but are playing the drums in tune. They just want to worship too.

When we define what those needs are within our local church and the community, we should begin establishing groups to help support the unique needs of individual and families. We must always remember that what affects one should impact all of us. We are all part of the inclusion team at church and beyond. It is what we do as individual Christians, or co-workers with others, that will make a difference in helping to create a stigma-free environment.

The church must develop a pastoral leadership team that is ever learning, creative, endeavoring to serve everyone at the highest capacity, equipping all the saints, building ministry teams, training volunteers to identify mental health challenges, and always updating ministry practices that better serve the people God brings to us. If we desire a stigma-free environment at church, we must adopt a mental health inclusion plan that works best for everyone.

Developing pastoral practices and a healthy church environment that welcomes people who struggle with mental health issues requires vision, awareness, intentionality, and wisdom, but every effort a church makes, both great and small, offers new hope and practical help to the silent sufferers among us. Hosea 4:6 says, "My people perish because of a lack of knowledge." Blessings to all in Jesus' name.

# ABOUT THE AUTHOR

DR. B.R. REESE. is a humanitarian and is passionate about caring for all people. He has been in pastoral care for over thirty-five years and has devoted many years of service to working with children in foster care and the underserved. Dr. Reese is a graduate of Granger ISD. He also attended Southwestern Baptist Seminary, Liberty University, and Austin Community College. He has a doctorate in theology from Evangel Christian University.

Dr. Reese is actively involved in the African-American community around mental health issues. He has worked with the African American Behavioral Health Network (ABHN), Faith-Based and Disability Initiative Central Texas (AAFSC), Alliance for Greater Work, Wellness, and Empowerment Community Ministries (WECM), Life Steps Council on Alcohol and Drugs, Austin Travis County Integral Care, A World for Children (AWFC), and many other organizations. He is also a member of Wilco Mental Health and serves as a board member of Pavilion Club, a mental health transitioning nonprofit organization.

While pastoring and doing public presentations, he experienced his own mental health challenges. He acknowledges that the Lord has taught him a valuable lesson; we all need non-judgmental, compassionate people around us. Reese believes stressors and mental weaknesses are no respecter of persons—anyone of us can experience a weak moment.

Reese is reaching out to pastors, church leaders, congregants, and beyond to get involved in their own personal recovery, becoming the path makers and pathfinders for a stigma-free church. He believes social networking among congregants and the community can be key for mental health healing at church and beyond. To that end, he has provided self-help tools and talking points that address a healthier dialogue around mental health in the church

Dr. Reese understands that all believers seek healing and understanding. He believes that when congregants and leaders face their challenges together, they are stronger in the healing process, and above all, we resemble a Christ-like church. Reese often asks this challenging question to pastors and leaders: Is your church a safe and healthy place to address mental health?

# ENDNOTES

1   http://hogg.utexas.edu/gods-way-faith-based-initiative

2   http://hogg.utexas.edu/churches-hurricane-harvey

3   https://www.nami.org/Find-Support/Diverse-Communities/African-American-Mental-Health

CPSIA information can be obtained
at www.ICGtesting.com
Printed in the USA
BVHW071105130819
555662BV00016B/2286/P